Toni Morrison and the New Black

Toni Morrison and the New Black examines how Morrison explores the concept of the new black in the context of post-soul, post-black and post-racial discourses. Morrison evolves the new black as symbolic of unprecedented black success in all walks of life, from politics to the media, business and beyond. Jaleel Akhtar's work shows how the new black reaffirms the possibility of upward mobility and success, and stands as testimony to the American Dream that anyone can achieve material success provided they work hard enough for it.

Jaleel Akhtar is Assistant Professor in English Literature at COMSATS, Lahore. He completed his DPhil from the University of Sussex under the supervision of Maria Lauret and Douglas Haynes in 2015. He is the author of *Dismemberment in the Fiction of Toni Morrison*, shortlisted for the Toni Morrison book award in 2015.

Toni Morrison and the New Black

Reading *God Help the Child*

Jaleel Akhtar

Routledge
Taylor & Francis Group
New York London

First published 2019
by Routledge
605 Third Avenue, New York, NY 10017

and by Routledge
2 Park Square, Milton Park, Abingdon, Oxon OX14 4RN

First issued in paperback 2021

Routledge is an imprint of the Taylor & Francis Group, an informa business

Library of Congress Cataloging-in-Publication Data
A catalog record has been requested for this book

ISBN 13: 978-1-03-209526-4 (pbk)
ISBN 13: 978-1-138-59138-7 (hbk)

Typeset in Times New Roman
by Apex CoVantage, LLC

For my all-caring mother Um-e-Kulsoom, my spiritual mother Chloe Wofford aka Toni, Toni Morrison. And the other-mothers in my life, Shereen Ghias, Maria Lauret, Marianne Mailie, Doreen du Boulay, and Mar Gallego.

Contents

Acknowledgments

First of all, I would like to thank Mike O'Driscoll from the University of Alberta for giving me the initial feedback on this project. I am especially grateful to him for reminding me that my discussion of the new black should not be disconnected from the political reality of contemporary US racial politics. I am also highly indebted to Paul C. Taylor for sharing his knowledge and expertise on the new black aesthetics. His encouraging remarks showed me I was moving in the right direction and "poised to tell a provocative story" with the help of thinkers like Hoyt Fuller and Trey Ellis and artists like Pharrell Williams. My deepest thanks go to Juda Bennett for his invaluable advice on not confusing post-racialism (which has run its course) with the new black and how "social forces" shape the new black's rise to success. I was lucky to enjoy his company at the Seventh Biennial Conference of the Toni Morrison Society in July 2016, held in New York, and felt tremendously supported by his feedback. My heartfelt gratitude goes to Mar Gallego for her helpful response and endorsement of my project as a promising domain of inquiry. I want to acknowledge Marianne Mailie with great appreciation for her unconditional support and feedback. The real impetus for the idea of this book came from the Toni Morrison scholars with whom I had the opportunity to share some of the ideas at the Seventh Biennial Conference of the Toni Morrison Society. I am particularly thankful to Rhone Fraser, Helena Woodard, La Vinia Jennings, Justine Tally, Evelyn Jaffe Schreiber, Farah Jasmine Griffin, and Herman Beavers.

The MS students at COMSATS Lahore who were keen to learn about Morrison and especially interested in reading and working on *God Help the Child*—in particular, Arooma Kanwal, Rabea Saeed, Mariam Fatima, Tahoor Ali (who also co-authored an essay on Morrison's *Jazz* with me), and Habib-ur-Rehman—all brought their own insights and honed my understanding of *God Help the Child*, while I was still working on this book. I am also indebted to my Panjab University mentors Prof. Shaishta Sonnu Sirajuddin (especially for inculcating in me a love for poetry), Ms. Shirin

Rahim (for opening the world of literature like an atlas) and Ms. Zareena Saeed (for introducing Ms. Morrison).

My deepest thanks are owed to my mentors at Sussex, Nicholas Royle (how nostalgic I feel about him), Maria Lauret (how desperately I wanted to say "let's do Morrison again"), and Douglas Haynes (for his faith and trust). I miss them all. A special debt of gratitude goes to my colleague Maqsood Ahmed, for his warm welcome home, to my friend Abu Baker Ghias Ali, and to my faculty mentor and esteemed director Qaisar Abbas at COMSATS Lahore. Thanks to Doreen du Boulay for her excellent help with the manuscript, my Routledge editors Jennifer Abbott and Veronica Haggar and the project manager Sheri Sipka for their professional expertise, friends, family, and other intellectual partners: Ninder Toor, Tajinderpal Singh, Yugvir Singh, Uzma Jabeen, Yvette Russell, Ayesha Aziz, Mariam Zia, Dr. Zulfiqar Hyder and family, Imran Khan and his family, Salman Rafique, Nabbiya Mubaraka, Asam Waseem, Khaleel Ahmed, Qasim Waseem, Naeem Akhtar, Ismail Masood, Farid-ud-Din, Shazia Maqsood, Dr. Muddassar Mahmood Ahmed, Dr. M. Mirza Zubair, Noor-ul-Hira, Iqbal Baryar, Asif Ikram, Mumtaz Dhanani and family, Irshad Dogar, and Dawood Ahmed.

Final thanks to my wife Fouzia Jaleel Akhtar for her patience, understanding and cooperation and to my little starlets Danish Ali Akhtar (for bringing joy and maturity to my life) and Hassan Ali Akhtar (for his contagious smiles).

Toni Morrison at the Seventh Biennial Conference of the Toni Morrison Society—
July 2016

Introduction

> The definitions of "black" and descriptions of what blackness means are so varied and loaded with slippery science and invention that it may be interesting [. . .] to examine the term's configurations and the literary uses to which they are put as well as the activity they inspire. . . .
>
> (Toni Morrison, *The Origin of Others*)

In *God Help the Child*, Morrison explores the concept of the new black in the context of the post-Black Arts, post-black and post-racial discourses. Like Alain Locke and his concept of the new negro, Morrison's new black values diversity by embracing contemporary concepts of (cosmetic) blackness and seeing race as extremely fluid; it offers new ways of thinking about gender, race, racial mobility and the construction of identity. The trope of the new black also helps us to re-evaluate the relations between the old and the new black subject positions. To borrow an expression from Margo Natalie Crawford, it involves a radical "'overturning' of fixed blackness" (*Black Post-Blackness* ch. 5). Morrison postulates her concept of the new black from the perspective of a young black woman with social aspirations, Lula Ann Bridewell, also known as Bride. She is a new role model who embodies the entrepreneurial spirit of the new black. Morrison's presentation of Bride allows her to redefine black identities, especially female sexuality, iconicity, economic success and social mobility. She is the site of black female sexual desire celebrating erotic agency. It is very rare to find black women writers who create a space in which black women explore the joys of the erotic and their sexuality, disclosing their intimate experiences without apology (Thompson L. 10, 71).

Bride, as the new black, is Morrison's answer to the feminist calls to foreground black women's "pleasure, exploration and agency" (Thompson L. 8). She is independent and socially mobile. She disregards the conservative rules of sexual conduct and respectability which could distract her from achieving agency, social mobility and greater financial success. Like Shayne Lee's description of the iconic black erotic revolutionary, Bride challenges the traditional scripts of black women which limit these women's sexual autonomy and encourages the new generation toward sexual agency and entitlement/empowerment (Lee "Introduction"). Unconcerned with the politics of respectability, which plays a pivotal role in constraining and policing the sexual behavior of blackness, she enjoys and experiments with a "mildly dangerous" sexual life (9), which makes room for a more expansive and fluid notion of blackness. Bride's celebration of her sexuality as a hidden resource of power is central to Morrison's construction of the new black. She gives expression to her sexual fantasies and autoerotic impulses without shame. Through her characterization of Bride, Morrison questions how black subjectivities are constructed (especially women labeled as bisexual or queer),[1] and how fluid and plastic such autoerotic sexual, androgynous, anorexic, and other gender and sexual orientations are. As the new black, Bride exemplifies the ability and strong nerve to achieve economic success, even at the cost of romantic commitment or fulfillment. During her early career, she finds herself at the bottom of the employment hierarchy because of her skin color, but she is tenacious and refuses to give up. As she carves out a successful career in business, she encounters white hierarchies and structures of power on her upwardly mobile way. In particular, she becomes the object of alliance, envy and prejudice and a source of professional rivalry for her white assistant, Brooklyn. Tracing the trajectory of her career, it is important to study the evolution of this phenomenal success from concepts like the new negro, the post-black, and the post-soul, which culminate in the zeitgeist of the new black.

The new black defines his/her subject position in terms of his/her material achievements. It reaffirms upward mobility and success, which is the promise of the American Dream. It stands testament to the American meritocracy that anyone can achieve material success provided they work hard enough for it. The rise of the new black can be read as the culmination and teleological achievement of the civil rights and post-civil rights eras (Fleetwood *On Racial Icons* 70–1). It has become a measure of racial success, especially since the post-civil rights era, which has seen the rise of iconic black celebrities in music, show business, entertainment, politics and business. As the new black, Bride shoulders, to use Baldwin's loaded expression, "the burden of representation," and the gendered legacy of the images of black (female) identity that encompasses the "weight and meaning of blackness for individual and collective racial bodies, and for historical, literal and symbolic bodies as well" (Dyson "Introduction"). It is befitting that Bride is born and raised in the nineties.[2] She comes of age in the twilight of a new black era marked by unprecedented black success in all walks of life, especially in the wake of the polarizing era of post-black and post-racial discourses, a period marked by the rise of the new black celebrity culture (Fleetwood *On Racial Icons* 58). In retrospect, the period covers the not-too-distant aesthetics of 1970s "black is beautiful" and its evolution into "black is the new black" (33). In fact, the black is beautiful sensibility of the black aesthetics anticipates the new black just as the new negro and the Harlem Renaissance anticipated the Black Arts Movement. The very fluid and hybrid nature of the new black is a manifestation of the black antici-patory aesthetics culminating in the burgeoning of multiracialism, which flowered in the first decade of the twenty-first century. The followers of this movement insisted on identifying themselves at the crossroads where black and white identities merge. Bride grows up at the confluence of these movements in the 1990s, which shape her identity (as the new black) and how we perceive it, making her part of the American melting pot. By cast-ing Bride (and the other characters in the novel) as the new black, Morrison anticipates how the fluid nature of blackness is appropriated, improvised and reclaimed in the 21st century.

Evolution of the New Black

I shall use the expressions post-black[3] and the new black interchangeably as both are by-products of a confluence of social forces, which draw their inspiration from the post-civil rights, post-soul and post-black power and black arts movements, to illustrate how this historical process has influ-enced the evolution of black people and their racial identities. It marks a shift in ideology and politics from the pre-civil rights to the post-civil rights generations. *Toni Morrison and the New Black* investigates the develop-ment of the new black as an evolutionary process from post-civil rights to post-soul to post-black blackness. In the wake of Obama's successful rise to the presidency, to be post-black has become synonymous with post-Obama, which means the post-black subject, like Obama, is "rooted in but not restricted by blackness" (Touré 12). Interestingly enough, as Derek Conrad Murray observes, the rise of the post-black or the new black coin-cided with the rise of Obama (Murray 19). Like the post-black subject, the new black does not consider himself or herself stymied by racism in his/her quest to realize his/her potential to gain material success or the American Dream. Convinced by his/her success, the new black, like the post-black subject, believes he/she has transcended racism. This carries the risk of color-blindness in not recognizing racial disparities and eco-nomic inequalities, which the new black might attribute to lack of motiva-tion or the inability to accept personal responsibility/failure (Winters *Hope Draped in Black* 157).

Cultural critics—Michael Touré and Orlando Patterson—caution against confusing post-blackness with post-racialism, which borders on color-blindness. In their eyes, the terms post-black and post-racial are not the same. They also emphasize that to be post-black or new black means the subject lives in a post-black ethos or is a product of this era. This implies that the definitions of blackness are expanding and there are multiple or infinite ways of experiencing blackness. As Touré claims, being post-black "does not mean we are leaving blackness behind, it means we're leaving behind the vision of blackness as something narrowly definable and we're embracing every conception of blackness as legitimate" (Touré 12). In other words, living in a post-black era offers limitless identity options or possibilities.[4] Being the new black now is being open to experiencing the full range and scope of blackness. Above all, post-black or the new black means, to borrow the expression from the artist Glenn Lion—who is credited with co-inventing the term "post-black" with the curator of Harlem Museum, Thelma Golden—"a more individualized notion of blackness" (qtd. in Touré 25). To expand this concept of individuation, the post-black subject or the new black is about agency, courage, "personal glamour," "sexual freedom," an insatiable thirst for success and, above all, individual pride in her/his achievements (79).

Bride is successful and pretty with an unflinching faith in personal enterprise. Like the black aesthetic slogan of "I'm black and beautiful!" she embodies the new black aesthetics as she derives satisfaction from her personal achievements: "I have what I've worked for and am good at it. I am proud of myself, I really am" (53). She believes in the work ethic, derives satisfaction from her physical endowments, and finds a source of racial pride within her own being. Like Alain Locke's new negro, she feels empowered from a more positive sense of "self-respect and self-reliance" (Locke *The New Negro* 10). She has carved out a successful career as an entrepreneur by challenging the systemic oppression of black people being offered limited opportunities in employment hierarchies. Like Locke's new negro, she wishes to be known for her accomplishments. Bride achieves her agency and individuality by capitalizing upon and wielding her blackness to her advantage, as we shall see. In her desire to achieve racial/social mobility, she successfully passes as the new black. The question of racial mobility is at the very heart of the concept of passing for the new black. It highlights the passer's struggles for freedom from the limitations of racial categories and forms of social oppression, as well as the passer's success in this endeavor.

The concept of the new black carries new cachet and significance, especially with reference to the tumultuous events surrounding racial politics in the US over the past few years, years which bore witness to mass protests by African Americans in response to the brutal and indiscriminate killing of innocent black youths like Michael Brown and Trayvon Martin.[5] The mass protests brought to the fore the racist policing practices in the United States, which makes the ideal of a post-racial epoch sound like utopia (Taylor K. "Introduction"). In face of the social injustice and indifference of the law enforcement agencies to the pain and suffering of African Americans, no wonder a new movement emerged and gained momentum, mobilizing the masses "to demand an end to rampant police brutality and murder against African Americans" (Taylor K. "Introduction"). It adopted the hashtag *BlackLivesMatter* and has been compared to the civil rights movement of the 1960s.

The emergence of this new movement in view of persistent racism and police brutality shatters the illusion of a color-blind, post-racial United States (Taylor K. "Introduction"). The nationwide protests, such as those in Ferguson, Missouri, have given added strength to the demands for justice and dealt a further blow to post-racial new black demands. The United States has been over-optimistically described as post-racial, while race is still a stumbling block on the way to upward mobility for minorities, especially Blacks, despite the example of Obama, which accounted for a "transformation of racial attitude and realities in the United States" (Taylor K. "Introduction"). Obama's presidency gave some validity to the currency of a post-racial, post-Obama era of racial politics (Frankowski 27). However, the example of Obama is not the only evidence of the transcendence of racism in the US. As Taylor observes, "thousands of Black elected officials, a layer of black corporate executives, and many highly visible Black Hollywood socialites and multimillionaire professional athletes animate the 'post-racial' landscape in the United States" (Taylor K. "Introduction").

The examples of all these successful Black professionals, like Oprah Winfrey, Serena Williams, Tiger Woods and Barack Obama—and the list goes on—are used to herald the post-racial era and to embody the spirit of the new black. The success stories of black professionals, who occupy positions of prestige and acclaim, reinforce the myth of post-racialism, which "imagines free and equal persons creating themselves, affiliating, and cooperating without regard for existing racial boundaries and scripts" (Taylor P. *On Obama* 33). But the dilemma of post-blackness or post-racialism is that the subject is still black. In fact, the subject is becoming more black as he/she experiences racism on a daily basis, and is reminded, to use the famous Orwellian expression, some are more equal than others. For example, despite Oprah's celebrity status and financial success, she still remains black and experienced racism while "shopping black"[6] during her visit to a posh handbag shop in Switzerland where the shop assistant refused to serve her, telling one of the richest women on earth that one of the bags was "too expensive" for her to purchase (Battersby).

Judging her on the basis of her skin, the shopkeeper refused to show her the expensive handbag as she considered her too poor to buy. Her fame and money does not help her avoid daily experiences of the racism that affect the lives of African Americans and blacks across the globe. bell hooks exercised uncanny foresight as she prophetically observed with reference to Oprah Winfrey that despite her powerful influence "as a producer and a performer," Winfrey failed to create the radical image of the (new) black for herself and for others (hooks *Salvation* 51). Winfrey's experience of blackness, her moment of epiphany, to use one of Morrison's favorite expressions, is no less humiliating than those faced by thousands of black shoppers who are hounded by security personnel solely on suspicion of being potential thieves.

Bride, too, experiences her own moments of blackness. A small episode, reminiscent of her early school days, occurs when she places an order for food at a restaurant on her way to find her ex-lover, Booker. The waitress treats her as if she had three eyes, despite Bride's rich appearance. Before finishing her meal, Bride feels the need to go to the ladies' room. She leaves "a five-dollar bill on the counter in case the waitress thought she was skipping" (81). The obvious allusion is to be black, new or old, is to be suspect. These factual and narrative anecdotes expose the fallacy of post-racialism and civil rights optimism that assumes black people can enjoy democracy, equality, freedom and live the American Dream like everyone else (hooks *Salvation* 62). As Juda Bennett astutely observed, "Morrison writes against the illusion that we have entered a period that is post-racial and that African Americans [. . .] have been freed from the social forces that have worked against their self-actualization" (*The Queer Pleasure* 152–3). Obama, who consciously and publicly identifies himself as the new black, has been no less a victim of racism than any other black celebrity. During Obama's first presidential campaign, his rival, Mitt Romney, attributed the former's success to the gifts he had showered on the minorities and illegal, undocumented immigrants. Obama was also made fun of by the then Italian prime minister, Berlusconi, for his suntanned skin, which was obviously a reference to the color of his skin. In 2016, the Republican presidential candidate, Ben Carson, cast doubt, like some other political rivals, about Obama's blackness. Carson claimed that Obama was "raised white," meaning Obama was not black enough to identify with the African American experience as, he, Carson, could, with his genuine African American parents, while Obama was born to a white American mother and a black Kenyan immigrant father. According to Carson, Obama spent most of his formative years in Indonesia, so he was cut off from the reality of the black experience and did not truly represent America as he, Carson, could. To add to this, Donald Trump questioned Obama's citizenship so much, starting the so-called birther movement, that the president had to officially release his birth certificate, and he further mocked the questioning of his citizenship at the 2011 White House Correspondents Dinner with the help of a video clip of Simba's birth celebration from Disney's famous *The Lion King*.

According to Eric Michael Dyson, "No other president has been so persistently challenged that he had to produce a birth certificate to settle the question of his citizenship" (5). Dyson further points out that two related but distinct racial charges were made against Obama: whether or not he is black, or black enough (36). According to Dyson, the first argument is "dressed in genes, even if it is also cloaked in social and cultural consequences" (36). The second argument is a "political judgement," questioning Obama's ability to empathize with the plight of black people. Such politically and racially motivated attacks put to rest the naïve optimism that Obama, with his ascent to power as president of the United States, had actually transcended racism. In fact, this highlights that the advent of post-racialism has been accompanied by "a shift in our racial practices," which makes it difficult to dismiss the notion that we have triumphed over racism. Like Morrison, Obama does not endorse the ideology of post-racialism and dismisses the notion that "we can get beyond our racial divisions in a single election cycle, or with a single candidacy" (qtd. in Taylor P. 35). However, despite such disavowals, in certain sections of society, Obama still managed to cut a post-racial figure because of his mercurial personality and expedient form of politics: "If black voters want to claim him as the black candidate, fine. If voters wanted to see him as biracial, or post-racial, that was fine, too" (Taylor P. *On Obama* 35). Obama embodies this fluid and multifaceted nature of blackness. Whereas post-racialism came into vogue after Obama's meteoric rise as the first black president, what actually makes him herald the concept of the new black is the example and precedence he set, which enables black people to draw inspiration and feel more empowered in terms of the ability to realize limitless potentialities. Bride embodies Obama's "Yes, We Can" spirit of the new black as a symbol of female empowerment. Like so many other examples of the new black to contemplate, black and other minority people can look up to Obama and say to themselves, "if he could achieve so much, why not me?" But as Morrison demonstrates in her fiction and nonfiction, the success of the new black or excessive faith in the realization of post-racialism and blackness is misguided. Skin color still remains a barrier to success. The white imaginary still enjoys the power to represent and engage in the commodification and objectification of the non-white or people of color. Behind Jeri's cultivation and projection of Bride as the new black in *God Help the Child*, there are the contributions and histories of other black celebrities and their commodification. Bride is a reincarnation that is part of a gallery of famous iconic black celebrities. There is the generation of previous black female celebrities from Josephine Baker to Dianna Ross and Grace Jones, to mention a few, who, like Bride, had limited access to education and material resources. All of them struggled for fame and success. *Toni Morrison and the New Black* investigates Bride's rise as the new black in the light of post-black discourses to demonstrate the resemblance she bears to her celebrity precursors, like Grace Jones, and how she, like them, contends with the "colour fetish" or "color-ism," which Morrison describes as "reminiscent of slavery itself" (*The Origin of Others* ch. 3).

Post-Black Is the New Black

Often misappraised, the new black is a highly provocative expression to use in this era of so-called post-black, post-Obama or post-racial blackness, despite the "posterizing" efforts to sublimate the old black to the new black, just like the efforts made by the proponents of the Black Arts Movement to sublimate the expression "negro" to "black" in an effort to claim racial pride and self-empowerment. The civil rights activists' struggle was to "turn Black from hated adjective to prideful noun" (Touré xv). Similarly, the new black is avant-garde and prestigious and aims at transforming the old discredited black into a source of pride and strength. Paul C. Taylor sees the black and post-black aesthetics in a continuum because the ideas conflate, coexist and influence each other. They are, in a sense, the forerunners of each other. According to Taylor, there is a considerable overlap between the "ideas of post-soul culture, post-civil rights politics, and post-black identity and aesthetics" (Taylor P. "Post-Black, Old Black"). Taylor's efforts to trace the term back to "post-soul" activists in the wake of the civil rights campaign was inspired by the curator, Thelma Golden, who used the expression to refer to post-civil rights black artists and their work for whom "the traditional meanings of blackness [. . .] are too confining. New meanings have emerged, new forms of black identity that are multiple, fluid and profoundly contingent, along with newly sophisticated understandings of race and identity" (qtd. in Mccaskill 178).

Margo Natalie Crawford has a similar opinion on the concept of "black post-blackness" (Crawford "What Was *Is*" 21). For her, it is "a way to understand the continuity between the BAM and twenty-first-century African American aesthetics" (Crawford "What Was *Is*" 21). For both writers, the posterizing concepts surrounding blackness are different names for a multiplicity of perspectives of the lived experience of the same complex reality. I shall employ these terms interchangeably because of the ambivalence and slipperiness surrounding their usage. There is also the need to look at how the post-black evolved into the concept of the new black. For example, Orlando Patterson observes, in his insightful review of Touré's *Who is Afraid of Post-blackness* entitled "The Post-Black Condition," that the term "post-black" "emerged only in the 1980s but by the 90s had become the "new black"" (Patterson). Quoting Touré, Patterson terms it yet another name for the complex and fluid state of being black: "a completely liquid shape-shifter that can take any form" (Patterson). It is again interesting to note how Patterson's opinion accords with the proponents of post-blackness in the art world, Thelma Golden and her friend Glenn Ligon. Talking about the post-black artists, the significance of their work and contribution, Golden avers:

> Their work speaks to an individual freedom that is the result of this transitional moment in the quest to define ongoing changes in the evolution of African-American art and ultimately to ongoing redefinitions of blackness in contemporary culture. . . . At the end of the nineties Glenn and I began, more and more, to see evidence of art and ideas that could only be labelled (both ironically and seriously) in this way—post-black. . . . In the beginning there were only a few marked instances of such an outlook, but at the end of the 1990s, it seemed that post-black had fully entered into the art world's consciousness. Post-black was the new black.
>
> (qtd. in Touré 32)

Golden uses the lexicon post-black as a shorthand for post-black artists and their work (Murray 4). However, the scope of post-blackness has been stretched by the post-civil rights generations looking for new expressions of self-definition in "an effort to redefine the parameters of blackness in the twenty-first century" and to reform the cultural, intellectual, political limitations and the aesthetics of pre-civil generations (Murray 9). For Touré, the term post-black is highly suggestive. According to him, "It clearly doesn't signify the end of blackness; it points, instead, to the end of the reign of a narrow, single notion of blackness. It doesn't mean we're over blackness, it means we are over our narrow understanding of what Blackness means" (Touré xvii).

Different terms like post-soul, post-black and the new black offer a window onto the artistic, sociocultural, political achievements and multifaceted evolution of black life from the civil rights movement to the new millennium. The concept post-black became a more fashionable designation, especially with reference to the new wave black artists who were more mainstream than their predecessors. It revolves around notions of blackness which occupied earlier generations but was adopted and transformed by the later generations into new shapes. Since these artists experience race differently, their work aims at redefining the complex notions or parameters of blackness in the twenty-first century (Murray 9). For these artists, the traditional notions of blackness have undergone a radical change; blackness has become more destabilizing and offers multiple possibilities and experiences of being black.[7] According to Paul C. Taylor, "to be post-black is to experience the contingency and fluidity of black identity, to have to wrestle with the question of how to orient one's self to the similarly fluid meanings and practices of the wider society" ("Post-Black, Old Black"). How does the concept of post-black artists in late the 90s differ from a contemporary take on the new black by artists like Pharrell Williams and Toni Morrison? *Toni Morrison and the New Black* contends that this concept of post-black blackness is not new to Morrison and that her fiction is replete with representations of new blacks who have achieved material success and upward mobility although they may not necessarily have celebrity status or an aura of "personal glamour" like Bride. For example, Milkman's father, Macon Dead, from *Song of Solomon*, who owns a lot of property and can bend the law in his favor because of his money, smacks of the condescension and snobbery typical of the new black in looking down upon his own family and people. Proud of his material achievements like the new black, he conveyed this message to his people: "I am not responsible for your pain; share your happiness with me but not your unhappiness (277)". In *Love*, Bill Cosey's resort is the source of racial pride and a symbol of black achievement for the black neighborhood (Fultz 96). People feel "a tick of entitlement" although the owner of the resort excludes the very same people from enjoying his premises that the hotel depended on for its life (42). As bell hooks observes, the rise of material prosperity amongst black folks caused them to become more self-centered; they stopped caring about other people or their material needs, and above all, the mutual love, respect and responsibility they had for each other, which used to be "a primary gesture of love" (hooks *Salvation* 26–7) ceased to exist.

Morrison's fiction critiques materially prosperous black people as representatives of the new black who are interested in money and success but not in the love ethic. In fact, their interpersonal relationships are capitalistic, exploitative and utilitarian. Thus, Morrison's take on the new black in *God Help the Child* is more complex and multifaceted. Her concept of the new black is not limited to the iconic blacks who represent the upwardly mobile. She writes about the queerness of identities and malleability of the black body, in fact, all the bodies, which brings a whole range of debates on black embodiment, black aesthetics, post-blackness and the new black. For example, the two central characters, Bride and Brooklyn, deliberately appropriate features of blackness and whiteness—clothes and hairstyles— as a way of embracing blackness or whiteness in order to achieve upward social mobility. Their crossover identification can be interpreted as a progressive act of cultural appropriation. In her essay, "Black Hair/Style Politics," Kobena Mercer reads hair as symbolic of the "creolizing cultures" of America: "some contemporary hairstyles among white youth maintain an ambiguous relationship with the stylising practices of their black counterparts" (Mercer 125). Beyond the act of cultural appropriation and ambiguous relationship, the cross-racial identification between Bride and Brooklyn can also be read within the dynamics of power relations and the aesthetics of the new black. Trey Ellis rightly foresees the appearance/arrival of the new black who celebrates the new black aesthetic or blackness from the vantage point of the cultural creole or mulatto who appropriates aspects of identities not considered authentically either black or white ("The New Black Aesthetic" 235). Both Bride and Brooklyn pass for each other by appropriating each other's cultural appearance. Both of them put the twenty-first century passing of black or white into conversation with each other. They seem to imitate each other and embrace aspects of American identity not authentically their own. Like the twenty-first century new black, they "celebrate exposure to and affinity for black and white cultural influences" (Thompson L. 127). Both appropriate identities at a time when creolization, multiracialism, cross-cultural borrowing, crossover and transracial identities have become apt terms for the new black aesthetics (Dreisinger 124). If both are laying a claim to a certain culture, i.e., whiteness or blackness by their appearance and social coding, both are vying for upward mobility. They become the embodiment of the contemporary representation of "transraciality" or cross-cultural appropriation. Michael Awkward defines transraciality as "the adoption of physical traits of difference for the purpose of impersonating a racial other" (qtd. in Dreisinger 41). Both characters can be read as examples of the new black, who exude cross-racial desire and crossover sexual attraction for the heterosexual men lusting after fair-skinned women with the blond dreadlocks associated with black women, and black women appropriating the silky curls, associated with blonde women, in order to succeed, thus creating competition between women of different colors. Jeri's mystifying statement "black is the new black" and the need for other women to "strip naked" in order to vie for attention can be understood in the context of this kind of competition.

The nurse who deals with Bride after her car accident is startled at the sight of the two of them: "one white girl with blond dreads, one very black one with silky curls" (23).[8] For the nurse, it is a moment of racial uncanny. Their physical and racial masquerade destabilizes her perceived notions of race and racial categories. Like the reader, her familiar racial identities are radically transformed into unfamiliar ones (Dreisinger 8). Morrison presents both of them as the new black, who embody some aesthetics of the new black, having to do with choice of their respective lifestyles. They romanticize and emulate each other in an effort to transcend their race or their skin color. The efficacy of their act of passing resides in their ability to demolish racial prejudices and stereotypes by establishing avenues of cross-racial understanding. The nurse is shown as a victim of skin consciousness, unable to see past the skin on which the novel puts so much emphasis. Bride ponders about why Brooklyn had "twisted her hair into dreadlocks" long before she met her. It was to "add an allure she wouldn't otherwise have. At least the black guys she dates think so" (44). Brooklyn's desire for interracial love, combined with her acts of cultural appropriation, reflect her desire for blackness, which she acquires through sexual intimacy with black men. If Brooklyn is trying to appropriate dreadlocks to appeal to black guys, is Bride not trying to adopt the model of beauty in the white male-dominated society, associated with silky and curly haired blondes? Her boyfriend, Booker, who is "simply dumbstruck" by the "knock-down" beauty of Bride, finds himself amused with her "insistence on white-only clothes" (133).

The strange power of embracing transracial and transcultural features is the hallmark of the new black aesthetics. These two characters can be read as the new black racial iconoclasts who shatter the taboos of interracial sex and the myth of racialized women who dared to have sex outside the boundaries of normativity, in the sense of having sex with members of the opposite racialized group. For example, blondes were racialized as "Nigger-lovers" for seeking black men, while black women were considered depraved and, in fact, punished like Sula for sleeping with whites. The racialization of these women was considered pathological and non-heteronormative. Morrison's new black—through her act of cross-identification and sexual proximity to the opposite race as in the case of Brooklyn—questions such heteronormative codes of behaviors. In fact, the subject positions of these women are those of passing women who desire blackness or whiteness by way of having sexual bonds with black men or vice versa. The new black is more liberated and entitled to sexual freedom without the fear of being judged or shamed even if his or her sexual orientation falls outside the boundaries of what society considers as normative behavior.

According to Derek Conrad Murray, the post-black is "inherently heterosexual" (18). Although *God Help the Child* celebrates the heterosexual relationship between Bride and Booker, the story questions this concept of post-black normative heterosexuality. Morrison's concept of the post-black blackness or the new black is queerly/holistically oriented. It is an expansive concept embracing all aspects of black experience that do not fall under the auspices of normative blackness, and this includes both closeted and uncloseted (black) sexualities. Expanding upon Thelma Golden's formulation of the post-black, it is more than an umbrella term signifying the burden of black experience; it becomes "a more pointed reference to a particular *regime of representation*: specifically, the history of images depicting black [wo]men in the throes of collective resistance" (Murray 4–5). For Murray, this is exemplified "in images of the Black Panthers, clad in leather jackets and berets, as they stand in militant opposition to racial oppression" (5). For Joy James, "Panther women leaders [. . .] romanticized as icons, noted for a particular form of appearance tied to 'fashion,' skin color and youth [. . .] led to their commodification" (qtd. in Neal 35). Golden reads into the Black Power era's iconic clothing, like the black leather jackets, and big afros, "myths of uncontrollable aggression and rampant sexuality" (Murray 5). The post-black in Morrison's formulation also becomes the new black and belongs to a regime of reference, pointing out the history of images, specifically from the perspectives of women who become symbols of sexuality and willing slaves of fashion/accoutrements or what Kathryn Stockton describes as *martyrs to clothes*. What does it mean to be a martyr to clothes? According to Stockton, there is a certain sense of shame or debasement attached to clothes when instead of simply adorning, enhancing beauty, protecting the body or being a source of empowerment, they become a source of denigration making "the wearer of beautiful garments a martyr to clothes" (*Beautiful Bottom* 42). A person becomes a martyr to clothes when s/he gives in to the cultural imperative to wear a certain type of clothing, which can become the cause of suffering, humiliation or inflict psychic wounds and distort subjectivity (*Beautiful Bottom* 42). Jeri's strict regimental imposition of white-only clothes evokes a history of representation in which black racial icons were brought to the "world stage" by various designers, artists and producers, in their struggle to achieve individuated achievement. *Toni Morrison and the New Black* investigates the relationship between famous black icons and their handlers vis-à-vis the relationship between Bride and her designer, Jeri.

The New Black and Social Mobility

In *God Help the Child*, Morrison evaluates and redefines the imperatives behind the new black experience and aesthetics, especially from the perspectives of iconic black professionals like Pharrell Williams, whose success is linked to their economic position. In recent times, Pharrell breathed new life into the concept of the new black after he gave the following controversial statement in his 2014 interview with Oprah Winfrey: "The New Black doesn't blame other races for our issues. The New Black dreams and realises that it's not a pigmentation; it's a mentality (Elan)." Pharrell's statement resonates with Hoyt W. Fuller's account of the spirit of the revolutionary black artist. Fuller defines the new black artist as a new breed of militant activist who "has decided that white racism will no longer exercise its insidious control over his work" (Fuller 200). The spirit of Pharrell's new black also shares affinities with Thelma Golden's artists "who were adamant about not being labelled as "black" artists, though their work was steeped, in fact deeply interested in, redefining complex notions of blackness" (qtd. in Murray 4). Pharrell's version of the black experience is highly privileged and subjective. He seems to advocate the American creed of meritocracy or the notion that those who work hard enough are rewarded. Based upon a belief in personal exceptionality, it does not offer an all-inclusive account. It downplays and overlooks the role that systematic or institutional racism plays in oppressing black minorities and keeping them underprivileged. It argues that economic success is possible. If a person is materially disadvantaged or economically poor, it is because s/he did not struggle enough to realize her/his own potential. Black people do not enjoy full enfranchisement, not because of systematic oppression, unemployment, lack of education and other facilities, but because of their own inability to achieve socioeconomic success. Endorsing an unqualified belief in meritocracy helps some white people, like it does Pharrell, to ethically deal with the social failures of minoritism and absolve themselves from responsibility. According to George Yancy, "Under the illusions of meritocracy, people of color fail because they have failed themselves" (*Look A White*). Those who are at the bottom of the racial hierarchy are there because of their own actions/responsibilities. Structural racism is not to be blamed for personal failure. Such opinions belong to the contemporary ideology of color-blind racism seeking to justify racial inequality by blaming the victim. If a black man is an underachiever, it is because he is not hardworking enough or lacks the initiative to better his lot (Bonilla-Silva 73).

Obama, who is the single most prominent example of the new black,[9] presented a similar logic while discussing the overall plight and backwardness of Africa instead of acknowledging or critiquing the role played by US foreign policy or governance: "I am a big believer that Africans are responsible for Africans" (qtd. in Dyson 145).[10] Embodying the new black spirit, Pharrell claims, "Upward mobility, that is the promise of America, and because I have achieved—you can, too" (Stereo). Pharrell advocates this at a time when black inequality, unemployment and underrepresentation is at a record high. On top of this, he holds blacks responsible for their own predicament as a direct result of what Taylor defines as "lapsed personal responsibility" (Taylor K. "Introduction"). Such comments subscribe to post-racial thinking which asserts that racial disparities between white and black have little to do with structural racism. Pharrell fails to observe that confining black people to the domestic sector, low-income jobs and depriving them of education limits their chances of upward mobility. In fact, as William David Hart observes, "Constraining black mobility (fundamentally, the freedom to be, the freedom to move) is a consistent thread in American history" ("Dead Black Man"). Unless blacks are exceptional, like Pharrell, pro-establishment and pro-status quo, they are to be challenged, controlled, disciplined and marked if they are invasive. Pharrell's comments fail to consider the basic democratic principle of equal opportunities for all. Instead of blaming people for their lack of motivation, institutionalized racism or other structures of power based upon hierarchies that do not provide equal resources, opportunities, education and employment to all must be considered. If Pharrell was able to achieve fame and material success through the sheer force of his determination or inborn talent, this is not possible for the majority of African Americans who are deprived of basic rights and privileges and have to face structural racism on a daily basis in their efforts to achieve the merit-based rights of a good education, health care and employment. The constraints on black upward mobility have economic, political and social implications, as the case is with Bride. According to Taylor, the debate over the failure of black social mobility seeks to justify "the black experience as something that exists outside of the American narrative of unimpeded social mobility, the pursuit of happiness and equality for all: a way to exonerate the American system while simultaneously implicating African Americans in their own hardships" (Taylor K. "Introduction"). Taylor adds that "any serious interrogation of the history of Black life in the United States upends all notions of American exceptionalism" (Taylor K. "Introduction"). Pharrell's views take no consideration of the larger picture and historical reality of African Americans' social oppression.

Pharrell's statement seems to be partially inspired by Touré, author of *Who is Afraid of Post-blackness*. Touré believes that blackness is a limitation which people need to transcend in order realize their potential. Touré interviewed and quotes successful black entrepreneurs, media moguls, writers and other iconic black celebrities in order to emphasize that the potential and realization of blackness are infinite and not restricted by blackness. According to Stephani Li, Touré's notion of (post-) blackness, just like that of Pharrell's, is an "individualist representation of what it means be black" ("Black Literary Writers" 44). In other words, it is not collective. It does not embody a collective representation or affirmation of black reality and its potential. It should embrace the collective struggle of all black people for upward mobility and the fundamental rights of citizenship, not only refer to the select few who were able to make it to the top. It is also ironic that a plethora of black celebrities like Pharrell should play down the dangers of being black in an era of so-called post-black, post-Obama racial blackness or transcendence that has seen some of the most outrageous crimes of victimization committed against black minorities in the US, including the brutal murders of unarmed black men like the teenager Trayvon Martin—whose murder is evocative of Emmett Till's lynching. The death of Trayvon Martin and the recurrent killings of black youth by the police, in the context of post-black, post-racial movements, shatter "the painful illusions of post-blackness" (Yancy & Jones *Pursuing Trayvon* "Introduction").

Morrison exposes the fallacy of post-blackness/post-racialism in her interview with Charlie Rose, in the aftermath of protests and violence after the death of Freddie Gray in police custody in Baltimore. The interview was aired on April 30, 2015, shortly after the publication of *God Help the Child*, first published April 21 2015. In this interview, Morrison condemns the relentless killing of unarmed black youth by the police as acts of cowardice. From Morrison's perspective, the young, unarmed, black men running for their lives from the police but still shot and killed over and over again are the new black as victims of state violence. Like Angela Davis, Morrison examines the failure of the system to challenge and scrutinize the ways in which the "ideological power of the figure of the young black male as criminal" continues to emerge in the American imaginary and cause tragic incidents (qtd. in Yancy *Black Bodies, White Gazes* xxi). She questions the credibility, complicity, irrationality and (ir)responsibility of those who dial 911. The obvious allusion is to the irresponsible, in fact, criminal behavior of people, like Zimmerman, who subscribe to the cultural perception that blacks are dangerous. People like Zimmerman continue to construct the presence of the black body as suspicious and a site of criminality. Zimmerman dialed 911 upon spotting Trayvon in his vicinity. While Zimmerman was in conversation with the dispatcher over the phone, he perpetuated all the stereotypes associated with the so-called criminal and suspicious behavior of black people. His initial description was, "This guy looks like he's up to no good or he's on drugs or something. It's raining and he's just walking around, looking about" (Yancy & Jones "Introduction"). Zimmerman's further description to the dispatcher is evocative of the suspicious and criminal behavior associated with blacks: "he looks black" and wears "a dark hoodie" (Yancy & Jones "Introduction"). Being black and also wearing a hoodie serves only to add to the dangerous appearance of Trayvon, who is described by Zimmerman as a "walking about" and "staring" no-good layabout (Yancy & Jones "Introduction"). After racially profiling Trayvon, Zimmerman uses racially loaded expressions directed not only at Trayvon but all black people. Zimmerman's stalking of Trayvon and his subsequent death is a subject worthy of separate investigation. But the fact that Zimmerman was able to escape charges of racially motivated murder is another indictment of society that shatters the "painful illusions" of the post-blackness and post-racial myths.

In *God Help the Child*, Morrison critiques similar acts of racial profiling, the use of racially loaded language and other forms of racial and social injustice. Brooklyn describes Booker as a "predator" (59). She spots him "with a bunch of raggedy losers at the subway entrance. Panhandling, for Christ's sake" (59). On another occasion, she spots him "walking aimlessly in neighbourhoods" (59). Brooklyn's description of Booker loafing about is similar to Zimmerman's description of Trayvon's "walking around, looking about" and "looks like he's up to no good." Brooklyn's description is in sharp contrast to the real predator in the book, the pedophile, who enjoys the reputation of being "the nicest man in the world" (111). The manner in which the pedophile is "caught, tried and convicted of SSS, sexually simulated murder of six boys" (118), including Booker's brother Adam, after six years, is a travesty of justice (120). This travesty of justice is again evocative of Zimmerman's trial and conviction. Zimmerman was not charged with manslaughter although an affidavit was issued by the lead homicide investigator, Chris Serine (Yancy & Jones "Introduction"). The State Attorney's office and Police Chief Lee did not dispute Zimmerman's claim of self-defense under the Stand Your Ground Law. In addition, Zimmerman was not examined to see if he was under the influence of drugs or alcohol. By contrast, an autopsy was performed on Trayvon's body to confirm the traces of marijuana in his body. A parallel case of similar police incompetence can be read in the scene of the police investigation after Adam's body is discovered. Upon request for help, "the police responded to [Adam's parents'] plea for help in searching for Adam, they immediately searched the Starbern's house—as though the anxious parents might be at fault. They checked to see if the father had a police record. He didn't. "We'll get back to you," they said. Then they dropped it. Another little black boy gone. So?" (113–4).

The narrator of *God Help the Child*, like Morrison the author, seems to lament the continual murder or disappearance of black youth followed by police incompetence. Faced with the disposable murders of black youth, Morrison calls for reform and the training of police forces in her interview with Rose. She bemoans the absence of black leadership, unlike in the days of civil rights, when black communities had leaders who could talk to the administration, mediate, and act as spokespersons or representatives of their beleaguered communities. She wonders if this were possible under Obama's leadership. Mike Eric Dyson seems to agree with Morrison about the lack of black leadership. According to Dyson, Obama failed to represent black folks as he was reluctant to raise his voice on issues of racism or address the commonplace acts of police brutality and seemed to downplay the concerns of the black populace "in order to reinforce his racial neutrality" (Dyson "Introduction"). The indiscriminate killing and brutal treatment of black people, especially by law enforcement agencies like the police, instantiate the prevalence of structural racism which has subjected black people to white violence since the days of slavery. Morrison, like the artist Glenn Ligon, cautions against the blind pursuit of individual instead of collective destiny in what she describes as "troubling and cowardly times" ("Interview"):

> I think we're getting beyond the notion of what collective blackness was. Blackness was about group definitions so there could be black leaders who spoke for black people in total. And I think we've moved beyond that and we're entering the space where more individualized conceptions of blackness will be the rule and not the exception. I think that's where we're headed.
>
> (qtd. in Touré 25)

In casting Bride as the new black, Morrison critiques the advocates of new black post-racial politics who downplay the importance of structural racial discrimination for the attainment of basic rights like education, employment, medical care, immigration and housing, etc. Their narrative of the post-racial/post-blackness or the new black fails to take into account the pernicious impact of racism on the daily lives of average African Americans, who are racially profiled and targeted. The new black, who celebrate their material success and enjoy their status, fail to observe that individual material success does not always mean social equality and social justice (Yancy *White on White* 179). To use Cornel West's popular expression, racism still matters and impacts on the lives of many people. According to Rone Shavers, "It matters not whether one subscribes to a pre-, post-, or ür-black idea of blackness, the fact that one possesses the biological markers for black will engender racist presumptions, however casual, naïve, or downright hostile" ("Fear of a Performative Planet" 89). For Morrison, the concept of blackness—old or new—provokes thoughts about race in multiple ways. Race is a marker of economic and political conditions. It is "a constant arbiter of difference [. . .] about power and the necessity of control" instead of being "the classification of a species [. . .] the human race, period" (Morrison *The Origin of Others* ch. 1). Above all, race is a social construct. It is "a by-product of a particularly racial form of power and subordination" (Murray 149). Morrison projects its power dynamics in the relationship between Bride and her design consultant, Jeri, who constructs Bride's identity as the new black through the complex dialects of power and domination, the gazer and the gazed, the definer and the defined, the colonizer and the colonized, the dominant and the dominated, the commodifier and the commodified. Above all, he constructs Bride's body from the vantage point of a capitalist who wants to transform her black body "from a marketable object, into a magical thing of desire" (Murray 55).

To this concept of the new black, which is loaded in the history of black commodification and its representation, Morrison incorporates a more contemporary and expansive notion of all those people who are socially and politically disenfranchised and find themselves at the bottom of hierarchies. This also includes Lana Guinier's and Gerald Torres' idea of a new black which "requires a redefinition of race that takes account of the broader historical moment we occupy" (Guinier & Torres 31). Although *God Help the Child* is Morrison's most contemporary novel in terms of its setting, it does encompass the broader historical moment. *Toni Morrison and the New Black* intends to explore the new black aesthetics in *God Help the Child* while tracing the trajectory of the old black aesthetic as exemplified in the Black Arts movement and Morrison's early fiction, like *The Bluest Eye* and *Sula*, written in the context of the black aesthetics and black is beautiful philosophy. Any understanding of the new black will not be complete without taking into consideration what the black aesthetic meant to its originators, how it underwent transformation, how it differs from the new black, and the location of the (new) black aesthetic in the realm of contemporary public debate (Martin 2). Thus, the concept of the new black inevitably begs the question, "What is the old black?" These are some of the intersectional questions *Toni Morrison and the New Black* seeks to address.

Becoming the New Black

The unwarranted faith in the American promise or dream that anyone can make it big verges on color blindness and perpetuates the myth that American society has its foundations in meritocracy. However, this is not the case, as Morrison has pointed out in her interviews, especially "The Pain of Being Black."[11] In this interview, Morrison identified inherent white privilege and supremacy as key to upward mobility, based upon the exclusion of minorities, the racialized other, especially the nigger. Being white or appearing to be white is the key to upward mobility. It resides in the conviction of "I ain't a Nigger," which Morrison claims to be the case for historical upward mobility in the United States: "Every immigrant knew he would not come at the very bottom. He had to come above at least one group—and that was us" ("The Pain" 255). She refers to European and fair-skinned immigrants, but implies people from all racial backgrounds and colors benefited from social climbing against blackness. The racialized hierarchy based upon color has kept black people at the bottom of the ladder, thereby preventing them from social climbing. In fact, blackness became a source of appropriation for white people to achieve their American Dream. Recently, Morrison has interpreted Trump's slogan "Make America Great Again" as "Make America White Again" at the cost of the eternally unassimilable other "me" ("Conversation"). It is through appropriating blackness that whiteness occupies "the top position within a vertical racialized social hierarchy" (Monahan *The Creolizing Subject* 24). The same applies to Latin American immigrants now. As a Puerto Rican sociologist Eduardo Bonilla-Silva observed, "When we come to the U.S. we immediately recognise whites on top and blacks on the bottom and say, 'My job is to be anything but black'" (qtd. in Guinier 19). From this perspective, upward mobility is based upon a degree of color hierarchy, a legacy of slavery and racism, which thrives upon blackness as long as it is at the bottom of that hierarchy. Being black meant being at the bottom of all hierarchies, social, political, economic, educational and employment: "the last one hired and the first one fired" (41).

Despite being the new black, Bride's hard work and talent and excelling in the business and fashion industries, and the overt and covert experiences of racism she undergoes, serve as a reminder of where she belongs in the class hierarchies or what hooks defines as "the color caste system," which defines American life. As the new black, she is open to the potentialities and dangers of the post-black experience, and this entails compromising the white gaze, "along with the added burden of disregarding the censoring black one" ("Patterson"). To disregard the black gaze, in Stephanie Li's opinion, is tantamount to ignoring the black ancestral presence in African American and Morrison's literature. This is simply not possible because African American literature is rooted in a benign ancestral presence and rejects "the unmooring of racial identity" (Li "Black Literary Writers" 45) that artists like Touré and Pharrell celebrate. Just like the new black artist, Bride wants to achieve upward mobility. She distances herself from her mother just like her mother distanced herself by training Bride to dislike her, and how her great grandmother distanced and cut herself off from her family and community of origin. Like the new black artist, she thinks that the source of success lies within rather than without. Along with material success comes the ability to look down upon others less materially advantaged. This is evident in the scene of Bride's rescue after her car accident in the novel (and the racist contempt she displays when she gets her maid, Rose, fired because "[she] could no longer stand the sight of [. . .] with cantaloupe breasts and watermelon behind" (57)). Bride is rescued by a white couple, Evelyn and her husband, Steve, who want to live a natural life devoid of material comfort. The conscious choice by the couple to say "no" to the comforts of a technologically driven modern lifestyle is looked down upon by Bride as a sign of their poverty. In an interesting role reversal, the couple, as the socially disenfranchised and underprivileged, become the new black and subject of disdain and ridicule for their lowly lifestyle. In

Bride's eyes, their poverty, as a reflection of their economic status, becomes an explanation for their social failure, for not having struggled hard enough like Bride to improve their lot.

Morrison's novels are cautionary tales about such individuals who disconnect themselves from their ancestors, genealogy, origins and history. Sula is an early example. Bride and Sula are like post-black sister sisters concerned with being (new) black. Morrison defined Sula "as quintessentially black, metaphorically black which is not melanin and certainly not unquestioning fidelity to the tribe. She is *new world black and new world woman* extracting choice from choicelessness, responding inventively to found things" (qtd. in Melancon 53). Melancon understands Morrison's rendition of Sula as the new black or an embodiment of the new world blackness which informs her female identity and sexuality. For Melancon, Sula's characterization is calculated as it illuminates "the often contradictory, resistive, subversive, and celebratory effects" and manifestations of blackness. The designation *new world*—whether pertaining to or qualifying *black* or *woman*—transcends a certain provincialism or absolutism that would resist blackness or black identity to the limited or territorial" (Melancon 53). Extracting choice from choicelessness comes closer to Patterson's definition of the post-black subject, upon the "liberating pursuit of individuality" (Patterson). Sula's tragedy is that she finds herself in pursuit of individuality society does not approve of, especially not at the cost of cutting yourself off from your community, ancestors or family. So being the new world or the new black does not mean the subject necessarily loves the members of his/her own family or community in his/her pursuit of happiness and social advancement. Morrison's fiction does not endorse the self-seeking pursuit of individuality. In fact, Morrison, like hooks, considers "Loving blackness [. . .] more important than gaining access to material privilege" (hooks *Salvation* 66). To borrow an expression from Morrison, the new black would not achieve "true maturity" if he/she stopped "caring unselfishly for somebody else" (*The Origin of Others* ch. 3), as she exemplifies it in Bride's unselfish act of risking her own life in defense of Rain.

The new world black attempts social advancement in order to enter the mainstream body politic, to attain first-class citizenship or privileges by severing the ties to her/his community, or by passing. Thus, passing or being white or belonging to a fairer complexion becomes the key to upward mobility. It is not entirely a way of rejecting blackness; it is a way of making sure you are not judged according to the values of the color caste system. In *God Help the Child*, the new black seems to challenge these hierarchies based upon complexion. For blacks and other minorities, American society is far from being a meritocracy where hard work pays off for those who are successful. The novel critiques social factors aiming to control and hinder black mobility. Morrison transitions the lived reality of being black from the old to the new black as she encapsulates the color-blind paradigms of post-racial, post-black and the new black. She deconstructs the new black and demonstrates once again how the myth of whiteness or fair complexion operate as a false transcendental "polarizing around it concepts such as purity, beauty, truth, right" (Yancy *I Don't See Color* 54–5). She exposes the social forces behind the construction of blackness and whiteness— whiteness as social aspiration instead of a mere color. She demonstrates how new forms of racism impact and upend the struggle to achieve upward mobility by the so-called new black. Bride faces challenges and racism before she succeeds as an entrepreneur. Jeri tries to discipline Bride. There is a power struggle between Bride and her assistant, Brooklyn, as the former threatens the racial status quo by becoming a successful new black business entrepreneur. Brooklyn dreams of replacing Bride at Sylvia Inc., where her position "might be up for grabs" (26).

According to Cynthia and Julie Willet, post-blackness (or the new black) revolves around the objective and subjective illusions of the entrepreneur and the dynamics of power struggles. The objective illusion sustains the belief in meritocracy "that work and talent drive the system" (Willet "Trayvon Martin"), whereas the subjective illusion convinces the subject that each individual has the potential to realize his/her entrepreneurial spirit. According to Cynthia and Julie Willet, this belief in post-blackness is tempting: "That is to say, good choices and hard work afford the cultural and professional skills to gain insider status, transforming blackness (in the experience of some) into a celebrated style, a fluid identity, and even a choice" (Willet "Trayvon Martin"). Such a conception of post-blackness suggests an African American or black can be a free agent (and not a product of capitalist system), but it would be naïve to think the post-racial era, marked by the (in)ability to sell blackness, is here. As Touré observes, to question someone is black (enough) or to question the authenticity of blackness "is to sell blackness short. To limit the potential of blackness. To be a child of lesser blackness" (5).

Jeri gives similar advice to Bride on how to sell her blackness. It is as if he is suggesting a legitimate way of performing blackness. He suggests to Bride a political and expedient way of embracing and cashing in on blackness. The success of black people depends upon the fluid nature of their blackness, whether or not they are black enough, and the extent to which they can manage to capitalize upon or sell their blackness to their benefit. When the business tycoon Rupert Murdoch claimed Obama was not a real black president and that America was still waiting for its real black president, he questioned whether Obama was black enough to understand the plight and suffering of black people.

Similarly, Morrison referred to Bill Clinton as being the first black president. Clinton's embracing blackness was an act of political expediency as he "shrewdly manipulated the meanings and symbols of blackness to his advantage," especially in order to gain the black vote (Dyson *The Black Presidency* "Introduction"). Morrison did not refer to Clinton's biological make-up or his vernacular. In fact, she meant he was black because of his "sense of fair play in the racial arena" (Yancy *White on White* 212). Morrison complimented Bill Clinton as being "our first black president," but the expression was metaphorical because Clinton, in Morrison's assessment, displayed "almost every trope of blackness: single-parent household, born poor, working-class, saxophone-playing, McDonald's- and-junk-food-loving boy from Arkansas" (qtd. in Li *Signifying* "Introduction"). To borrow an expression from Clarence Sholé Johnson, Clinton's signifying blackness was more political in the sense of being "subversive of the status quo, viz. whiteness. Given this use, there is no incongruity in the idea of being pigmentationally white and politically black, or a person being pigmentationally black and politically white. All it means is that she or he is ideologically committed to decentring whiteness; that she or he is oppositional or counterhegemonic" (qtd. in Yancy *White on White* 180).

Obama had his own way of capitalizing on his blackness or his biracial identity which made his career an unlikely success story. Because of his biracial identity, he could mediate and resolve racial tensions between groups from different racial backgrounds. The word biracial, as Dyson observes, is a significant "improvement over other terms that suggest interracial mixture, from quadroon to mulatto" (Dyson ch. 2). The novel *God Help the Child* refers to "all mulatto types and quadroons" (3) and what they did in the past and what they have to do in the present to survive and succeed in a society beset with the evils of color bias. All these character types, including the Oreo, are Morrison's improvement on what Juda Bennett describes as Morrison's *figure of the passer*. There was a time before being black became racially and politically loaded—"being black and loving Jimi Hendrix was like being black and loving hockey or country music: a curious sort of pursuit for somebody with melanin. Way back when there were few clearer signs of being black on the outside and white on the inside (the classic old stigma of "Oreo" African American) than declaring love for James Marshall Hendrix" (Walker *Black Cool* 133). Now being the new black has become fashionable (even if it means being Oreo or acting white). It is the new norm and its pursuit has become economic, intellectual and political. This pursuit of blackness raises a more basic issue: What does it mean to be black now or who is the new black, considering its fluid nature and ever-expanding boundaries? There is the famous case of Rachel Dolezal, of Caucasian ethnicity but who successfully passes for black or chooses to *become* black by identifying herself as black (in an apparent effort to achieve upward mobility). She was "'outed' as being a white woman passing for black" (Crawford *Black Post-Blackness* ch. 7). What are the ramifications for a white passing for black? Did Dolezal face any structural racism as a Caucasian in her efforts toward "upward mobility," like Bride does? Did she become black in order to advance her career and to enjoy certain power and prestige in society? If a Caucasian could identify herself as black and vice versa then what does race signify? Does it mean it is just a linguistic performative? Does that mean the concept of race is fast evolving or has become politically expedient? Or is she politically black like Morrison's Clinton who is racially anti-status quo, or like Pharrell, who wants to endorse and be part of the status quo? Normally, the desire to be white reflects a desire to occupy a position of power or to acquire certain privileges (Yancy *White on White* 178). Dolezal does not endorse adopting an expedient form of blackness, like putting on a costume or wearing a weave or Afro or dreadlocks, like Dolezal, to feel black in order to attain certain material benefits (Dolezal *In Full Color* 1). For her, being black is more than a matter of physical appearance: "It's the culture you inhabit and the experiences you've lived. It is philosophical, emotional, even spiritual" (*In Full Color* 3). So to be the new black like Dolezal is possible by empathizing with blacks or by experiencing being black. As a person who has an arguably white background but identifies herself as black, Rachel reverses the logic of being white as key to upward mobility and refutes the logic of the biological essence of blackness (Yancy *White on White* 182). An act of cultural affiliation, like Rachel's, as cultural theorists Kenneth W. Mack and Guy-Uriel E. Charles suggest, overturns the notion of fixed identities with an alternative notion of racial affiliation as a matter of "voluntary cultural affiliation" rather than a measure of economic success or biological/social difference (3).

Paul C. Taylor is more at ease with Morrison's claim that race is a social construct; "our social affiliations—including our ethnoracial affiliations—are not natural or fixed but contingent and can be chosen, or not [. . .] and that our main ethnoracial categories have never been and cannot be as pure and inviolate as we once pretended they were" (*On Obama* 16). This seems to be the case with Tiger Woods, whose statement of being "Cablinasian"—a blend word signifying a Caucasian, Black, Indian, Asian background—affirms the fluidity and protean nature of all racial identities. Morrison demonstrated the nature of such ethnoracial affiliations in *Jazz* and *Tar Baby*. Henry Lestroy and Golden Gray have a classic encounter where the father figure, Henry, asks his son, Gray, to choose his racial identity: "Be what you want—white or black. Choose" (*Jazz* 173). In *Tar Baby*, Morrison depicts the tension between "black is beautiful"—natural hair and dark-skinned blackness as the epitome of black beauty—and the characterization of Alma Estee as black drag, which can be read in the context of the novel as the emerging new black. Morrison contrasts the "midnight skin" of Alma with images of grotesque aestheticization. This has the impact of creating abject revulsion in the patriarchal sensibility of Son, who, conditioned by the Black Arts philosophy of black is beautiful, wants to tame and subjugate Alma's sexuality (Crawford *Dilution Anxiety* 101). According to Margo Natalie Crawford, "The red wig is a sign of artifice attached to the midnight skin, which Son believes is Alma's essence" (*Dilution Anxiety* 104), just like the white dress on Bride's "midnight black, Sudanese black" (3) skin works as a poultice and reflects a desire to duplicate white skin.[12] The dress exposes, as it were, the whiteness within. With artifice(s) attached to her skin, Son sees Alma as artificial and grotesque, like a "bougainvillea in a girdle," a "baby jaguar with lipstick on," and an "avocado with earrings" (299), instead of appearing as she "really was" (299). Alma appears to Son, with the artifice of the red wig, as unnatural, inauthentic and grotesque; Bride too appears artificial and inauthentic—a reflection of Jeri's grotesque imagination. The white-only clothes reflect the tension that exists between how she feels and how she appears, as an Oreo. Oreo becomes a classic du Boisean metaphor for her binary/double consciousness, outlandish appearance and split personality. Morrison's formulation/theory of the new black in her latest novel *God Help the Child* addresses the destructive impact of new beauty standards and how to remain natural without losing authenticity.

The Black Body and Its Handlers

The main focus of this project is the traumatic relationship between the white gaze of Jeri, who is Bride's consultant designer, and the black female corporeality of Bride, who embodies the role of the new black. Jeri is a successful design consultant, making sure that blackness sells. Bride consults him to manage her self-image and advance her career. He appraises her body on the occasion of her second interview for Sylvia, Inc., the interview which eventually launches her career as the CEO of *You, Girl* (possibly a pun on Elle Girl): "You should always wear white, Bride. Only white and all white all the time" (33). Jeri is an image-maker for Bride. His ability to create images to project the black body means that he not only occupies a position of power but also delivers the discourses that prevail and continue to construct the way we perceive the black body.

Whites have historically enjoyed the privileged status of being the "lookers" and "gazers" of the othered body and the site of power it occupies (Yancy *Black Bodies, White Gazes* xvii). According to Ishmael Reed, white men dominate the media. They enjoy total power and control as scriptwriters, television commentators, producers, directors and media moguls, and they define the black experience to its denigration and (dis)advantage (Reed 181–3). This insight links the subject of black embodiment and its representation to the Derridean concept of archival violence: how the black mind is externally constructed like an archive. For example, Jeri's construction and representation of Bride's body continues the archival violence of the fashion industry as he determines how best she can display her black body to her (dis)advantage. Jeri's projection of whiteness onto Bride—in his effort to enhance her exotic beauty—is evocative of certain famous bodily performances/representations by iconic ethnic or Afro-American artists, stylists and models like Naomi Sims, Dianna Ross and Grace Jones, who were precursors of each other and represented the famous slogan of black is beautiful in their own unique manner. As Elaine Scarry observes, the question of beauty "prompts the mind to move chronologically back in search for precedents and parallels, to move forward into new acts of creation, to move conceptually over, to bring things into relation" (Scarry 30). Therefore, it is important to study Bride in relation to her precursors like Sarah Baartman, Josephine Baker and Grace Jones. Although the iconic, the mythical and the stereotypical representation of black female sexuality continued to proliferate, starting from Baartman, also known as the Black Venus or the Hottentot, throughout the nineteenth and the twentieth centuries, it was embodied and enacted in real-life by entertainers like Josephine Baker as the African American sex goddess, whose reincarnation was relived decades later by celebrities like Grace Jones. What is strikingly similar about the black professionals (and Bride) is the relationships that existed between these black women and their exhibitors, handlers, and consultants who were bent on displaying their bodies or their bodily representations as exotic animals.

In order to find "precedents and parallels" between black icons and their handlers, *Toni Morrison and the New Black* involves scholarship not only on Morrison, black aesthetics, post-racial theory and other cultural representations of race and gender, but also the visual representations of black women in the media, culture, pop music, beauty pageants and the photographic/visual archives which depict blacks through visual caricatures and stereotypical roles, and their harmful impact on a Morrison character like Bride. I will look at how men as image-makers, cultural agents and fashion designers continue to construct images of black women as fetishized, marketable commodities and cultural symbols; how the archives of black beauty pageants continue to perpetuate violence on women's bodies by investing in images of exoticization to enhance their sexual appeal and in the case of Morrison's most recent characters like Bride, their Oreoness. Finally, the book traces the development of the concept "black is the new black" along a continuum with the aesthetics of African American blackness in its entirety—covering the Black Arts movement, black power movement, black is beautiful and the post-black or post-Obama schools of thought.

God Help the Child is divided into four parts and so is my discussion of this deceptively simple novel. Each part of the novel is different from the other in terms of its length and narrative perspectives or sequences, Part I being the longest. Most chapters are named after an individual character and the narrative events are voiced or narrated from his/her perspective. The narrative perspectives are mainly from "the first-person narrations of different characters" (Goldberg) but a couple of segments from Parts II and III and one segment from part 4 are unnamed and vocalized through a third-person narrator. Morrison develops her story using both the classical tradition of passing narrative and the contemporary one of passing paradigms. From the "Black is beautiful" aesthetics to "Black is the new black," my discussion of the novel seeks to link the paradigms of passing narrative and the evolution of the old black aesthetics into the new black.

Chapter 1 looks at how Morrison foregrounds the historical theme of passing. It captures the transition from the old black to the new and the paradigms of passing as the old and the new black. It looks at the medium of passing as an attempt at social climbing or upward mobility, whereby black people tried to cross the color line to assimilate themselves into the more privileged and mainstream white society. The history of passing in Sweetness' family is a commentary upon African Americans' struggle to pass for white in order to have better employment and to achieve greater social mobility. It looks at the enduring relevance of the passing motif, how it addresses the viability of race in this era of post-blackness and how Morrison's novels are interconnected through themes of passing. The chapter also investigates how interpersonal relations between mother and daughter, husband and wife become complicated and splintered because of colorism (color prejudice), racism and the imperative to pass. This chapter discusses Sweetness' hatred of her daughter in the vein of the traditional narratives of passing in which the too-black child—also described as the atavistic child—becomes the object of derision. Morrison's deployment of the trope of the black baby and her act of situating the tale, especially the birth and nurturing difficulties of Lula Ann, in the 1990s—the so-called era of neo-liberalism and the peak of multiracial movement—grasps the challenging issues of identity crisis. One of the objectives of this chapter is to help the reader understand how Morrison redefines the twenty-first century problem of colorism as a struggle to pass. It is important to look at this history of passing because Morrison links this desire to succeed to the theme of the new black in the upcoming chapters.

Chapter 2 focuses on the first-person narrative vocalized by Bride. It covers the scenes of her breakup with her boyfriend, Booker, her flare-up with Sofia Huxley and her problematic relations with her mother and her lover, Booker. However, Bride's interactions with Jeri, her image consultant and the power he wields, will be central to the discussion. This chapter studies Bride's relationship with her consultant, Jeri, in the context of the relationship between famous black models and celebrities like Grace Jones, Josephine Baker and their handlers, consultants or exhibitors like Jean-Paul Goude and Paul Colin to understand how Jeri views the tar-black body of Bride as exotic and grotesque at the same time. The purpose is to show how Morrison defines the ideal of beauty as a hierarchized relationship between black bodies and their handlers whom Morrison critiques as purveyors of exotic beauty and to demonstrate how Jeri emulates Jean-Paul Goude in his marketing of Bride by re-packaging her black body to reflect her Oreoness or internal whiteness. He does this by controlling her clothes, etc., and by presenting her as an object of exotic appeal. In *The Origin of Others*, Morrison observes that the stripped or "sparsely clothed" (black) body has been represented as an object of "undisciplined eroticism" instead of attention being focused on the voyeurism of the observer or the designer (ch. 6). The purpose of this chapter is to expose the voyeurism of Jeri as Bride's image-maker and the power he exercises by eroticizing Bride's body by projecting it as an object of exotic beauty.

Chapter 3 examines how Jeri, as a total concept-designer, takes a holistic approach and designs everything, i.e., clothes, jewelery and other accessories for Bride. It looks at how Jeri constructs the overall personality of Bride and how her black body becomes subject to the imposition of white beauty standards or values in dress code and appearance, totally subordinated to the choices if not prejudices of the "total person makeover" he gives her, assuming ultimate authority on dress code and external appearance. The black now—long emancipated and free—is an empowered subject. But traps exist for the new black—being black is to be black for the public and not black in itself or for itself. If the question is not about turning white or appearing white in terms of external appearance, it is still about living a life according to the white imaginary. It still entails a negation of the self or the internalization of a negative self-image, as with Bride. Dressed all in white like Grace Jones, she presents herself as an image of what she considers to be appealing to others. She internalizes whiteness so much that she not only wears white and eats white; she becomes mentally white. Finally, this chapter looks at how men as image-makers, cultural agents and fashion designers continue to construct the images of black women as fetishized, marketable commodities and cultural symbols; how the archives of black beauty pageants continue to perpetuate violence on women's bodies by investing in exoticized images, which enhance their sexual appeal, exoticism and, in the case of Morrison's most recent characters, like Bride, their Oreoness.

Chapter 4 looks at the impact of child abuse on the lives of Bride and Booker. I look at how Bride and Booker cope in their separate lives after their breakup. For example, I focus on the physical metamorphosis that Bride undergoes as a result of this emotional breakup. She thinks she is reverting to a prepubescent childlike state, to be the atavistic child who was a source of shame for her parents (97). Morrison dramatizes this state of regression through the disappearance of the "tiny holes" in her earlobes which look "virgin," "untouched by a needle, smooth as a baby's thumb," accompanied by the alarming realization that her armpits and pudenda have become hairless (57, 97), and the gradual downsizing of her body, including the breasts she would prize as the source of her empowerment and femininity (97). Her loss of hair becomes a metaphor for the literal loss or erasure of her agency/subjectivity and sanity. This chapter contends that most of her bodily transformation takes place at the level of hallucinations which trigger the loss of her bodily self-image, especially in the wake of Booker's desertion of her. This chapter examines Bride's quest to seek an explanation which eventually leads her to self-discovery and the restoration of her subjectivity/womanhood. Since part of the novel also revolves around Booker, his past life, his aspirations as a student, his family life and the loss of his favorite brother, Adam, a victim of child abuse, the discussion focuses on how Booker copes with his state of mourning or the melancholia which affects his family and interpersonal relations and how he finally overcomes his loss. Borrowing from David W. McIvor's concept of democratic mourning as a civic obligation or an open democratic dynamic, I argue that Booker's act of mourning embodies an ongoing democratic labor of recognition and repair in the face of ongoing experiences of social loss, trauma, violence, disrespect, devaluation of life, marginalization and other instances of social injustice. I argue that Booker's melancholy is part of an enduring legacy of struggle with racial oppression, abuse and violence. His melancholia demands justice and reparation not only for his brother but for the unaccounted-for black boys who also disappeared without trace, a demand for social justice and reconciliation toward the elimination of institutional racism.

The conclusion looks at the last chapter of the novel, which is narrated from the perspective of Sweetness. It is in the form of a plea, a prayer, an apologia or an apostrophe in which she takes stock of her accountability as a mother and the tremendous burden of having to rear her daughter in a racist society. Within the monologue is a mother-child dialogue. From the prayerful perspective of the mother, Morrison envisions a grammar of

responsibility from multiple angles: "Being responsible, holding someone responsible, taking responsibility, to have responsibility, and being a
responsible person" (Oforlea *James Baldwin, Toni Morrison* ch. 6). I argue
that the question of responsibility in prayer is central to the mother-daughter
dialogue/relationship. She questions her own behavior as a mother—which
experiences of racism made complex for her—in a self-reflective and critical way. Now that her own daughter, Bride, is pregnant, she addresses her
daughter in the vocative as she imagines the future of her daughter's child.
She ends her monologue on a salvific note in the form of a prayer and on a
note of hope, represented by the image of a child who embodies the hope,
promise, symbol and telos for global citizenship and identities.

Toni Morrison and the New Black looks at how Morrison's latest novel
God Help the Child expands upon the fluid and performative nature of
blackness. It argues that Toni Morrison's concept of the new black or the
new black aesthetics evolved from the new negro and the Black Arts Movement. Morrison's concept of the new black is an offshoot of "Black is
Beautiful" based upon aesthetics of improvisatory revision. Morrison still
envisions black aesthetics as expansive and performative of multiple identities and untapped potentialities. *Toni Morrison and the New Black* demonstrates how Morrison's black subject evolves and is refashioned in the
twenty-first century to expand the potentialities of black performance and
identities. The book argues that Morrison's notion of the new black pushes
the boundaries beyond any fixed definitions or notions of black subjectivities, offering an alternative version of multiple and fluid black identities.

Notes

1. Like the new black which encapsulates "women of all colour from ebony to
   lemonade to milk" (10), queer does not mean gay, but covers many aspects,
   like masochism, paedophilia, sadism, etc., as well as not growing up straight or
   upwards as Kathryn Stockton's expression of "growing sideways" suggests. In
   one sense, queer is the opposite of straight, but implies a lot more depending
   upon the context.
2. It is very important to note that Bride was born and raised in the 90s. According
   to Allyson Hobbs, beginning in the 1990s, American society started to recognize hybrid identities (*A Chosen Exile*). This change was reflected not only in
   personal attitudes but also in federal racial classifications (*A Chosen Exile* 274).
   By the late 1990s, people were comfortable with malleable, multiracial and
   hybrid identities. The first few years of 1990s till the first decade of the new
   millennium saw a watershed in national and international events that marked
   a new phase in history—a breaking of barriers, which set the stage for the first
   black president. The rise of the new black was the product of the multiracial
   movement, founded on the notion of breaking barriers, in 1990. For a further
   discussion of the 90s as a "watershed of national and international events" see
   Julie Cary Nerad's *Passing Interest* (5–6). The multiracial movement of the

90s, produced a significant shift in how we view race now (Nerad 70). The mixed-race author, Danzy Senna, refers to it as the "mulatto millennium," which *God Help the Child* defines as the age of the new black (Nerad 276).

3. For further discussion of the concept of post-black, see Derek Conrad Murray's excellent investigation *Queering Post-Black Art*. See also, Touré's *Who's Afraid of Post-Blackness* and *The Trouble with Post-Blackness*, edited by Houston A. Baker and K. Merinda Simmons. However, some of the best and most excellent scholarship on post-blackness is by Margo Natalie Crawford in her indispensable book *Black Post-Blackness* in which she defines "Black post-blackness as a holding on and letting go of blackness that requires a move beyond the assumption that playing with blackness is a betrayal of commitment to struggle against oppression" (ch. 7).

4. Consider Morrison's interview on the condition of being black with Bessie W. Jones and Audrey Vinson in the mid-1980s. Morrison anticipated the post-black and new black potentialities available to any person who chooses blackness as a matter of choice: "Being Black now is something you have to choose to be. Choose it no matter what your skin color" (186).

5. Brown and Martin are only two examples of the countless unarmed and slain young black bodies which make mourning an everyday feeling and part of the lived reality of being the new black. In fact, they shift the focus from successful black celebrities to the indiscriminate victims of the police and state violence who get no justice, or are potential targets of shootings by law enforcement agencies entrusted with protecting the very lives they take in open public spaces with impunity, throwing their loved ones into a perpetual state of mourning.

6. Oprah Winfrey discussed similar moments of racism, while dining black in New York, in her interview with Larry King entitled "We Are Having A Racist Moment: Oprah Discusses New Incident in NY," published on 5 Aug, 2013.

7. The post-black is not merely a nomenclature for post-black artists and their work, as Thelma Golden initially claimed. For me, post-black has morphed into the new black. It has become more global in its outreach and can be used to describe the social, political and cultural experiences of not only African Americans, but all oppressed people who empathize with African Americans and their social and political struggle for civil rights, justice, and liberation. See Molefi Kete Asante for an insightful discussion of blackness as a trope for universal consciousness that finds identification with the social and political struggle of African Americans for their liberation ("Blackness as an Ethical Trope"). Thus, the concept of the new black has become transcendent to describe the plight of disenfranchised and suppressed minorities anywhere in the world. Morrison's depiction of Huxley "gobbling like a refugee, like somebody who's been floating at sea without food or water for weeks" (18) captures the predicament of world refugees forced to take perilous sea journeys. This description, with all its visual power, is reminiscent of the three-year-old Syrian refugee boy Alan Kurdi whose dead body was driven ashore on a Turkish beach. As Janine Jones argues, it is possible for non-blacks to experience certain forms of blackness without being black. Jones gives the example of the Palestinian poet Suheir Hammad, who entitled one of her works "Born Palestinian, Born Black" because as a poet, she could empathize with the "political, social, cultural, aesthetic, and economic condition of being black, where being black represents, across these parameters, being at the *very* bottom" ("Tongue Smell Color" 231).

8. Consider Janelle Hobson's description of Madonna's attempts at "blonde ambitions" in *Body as Evidence*. According to Hobson, Madonna tries to copy the most celebrated blondes like Marilyn Monroe—the symbol of ultimate blonde—and Lady Gaga, who are natural brunettes. She adds that blonde hair on Madonna is "not so easily recognisable as artifice, due to her white body, as [it] become[s] obvious via the black body that dons blond hair and other white feminine signifiers" (51). Thus, it is the acts of "racial appropriations" which highlight the artifice (51) or the subject's attempt at passing for someone else.

9. According to Kenneth W. Mack and Guy-Uriel E. Charles, the need to define "the new black" became more pressing, especially in light of Obama's success as the first black president of the United States (4). See also Stephanie Li, who discusses how Obama's reign transformed America's race relations in suggesting the country had become at least post-racial (Li *Signifying* "Introduction"). Although Obama was never identified as post-racial or the new black, he certainly benefitted from race without directly speaking about race ("Introduction"). Just an aside here: Morrison was reportedly writing a novel on the life of a black president during the years she wrote *God Help the Child*.

10. It is very interesting to read this statement in comparison with Peter Downes' pro-slavery argument with Jacob Vaark in *A Mercy* (28–9). Such argument wears "the garb of a disguised apology" (Akhtar 7).

11. Morrison has exposed the structure of hierarchies based upon color lines or skin privileges in her fiction and numerous interviews, including her famous essay "Home" in which she critiques the ideology of post-racialism as a utopian fantasy.

12. Margo Natalie Crawford offers not only some of the most enlightening insights into black aesthetics, the Black Arts Movement and the post-black aesthetics, but her discussions of Morrison's *The Bluest Eye* and especially *Tar Baby* in her masterpiece *Dilution Anxiety* and *Black Post-Blackness* can also offer the key to understanding *God Help the Child*.

1 Passing as the Old Black

Almost all mulatto types and quadroons did that back in the day [. . .] My own mother, could have passed easy, but she chose not to. She told me the price she paid for that decision.

(God Help the Child)

A reader familiar with Toni Morrison's style and themes cannot fail to observe similarities between her new novel, *God Help the Child*, and her previous novels, starting from *The Bluest Eye* and *Tar Baby*, to her later *Love* and *A Mercy*. In her early novels, like *The Bluest Eye*, *Song of Solomon* and *Jazz*, Morrison critiques "the harmful effect of the beauty industry" (Stern). In *The Bluest Eye*, Morrison responds to the Black Arts and Black Power movements' nationalistic slogan of "black is beautiful," which Morrison describes as "a white idea turned inside out" and one of "the most destructive ideas in the history of human thought" (Stern). *God Help the Child* offers Morrison's new take on black is beautiful, and the political import of the new black aesthetics, which ranges from post-civil rights, post-soul and post-black to the new black discourses. She rejects, like the proponents of the Black Arts Movement, the classical concept of art for art's sake, as she exposes new forms of nuanced racism and child abuse—a theme she seems to carry forward and develop from *Love*. Morrison continues to expose the process of racialism as an aesthetic project, especially in its evocation of black iconography and a racialized construction of the black body as exotic and glamorous. According to Margo Natalie Crawford, Morrison's fiction demonstrates the aestheticization of human beings, especially that of black body, as problematic if not impossible (*Dilution Anxiety* 96).

The philosophy of black is beautiful was at its height and the driving force behind Morrison's first novel *The Bluest Eye*, written "during the full span of the Black Arts movement, between 1962 and 1970" (Crawford *Dilution Anxiety* 19). In her new afterword to the novel, Morrison dwells upon the concept of black is beautiful or the Black Arts movement's idea of natural black beauty, which was "a key part of the body politics of Black Arts Movement" (Crawford "Natural Black Beauty" 154). According to Crawford, *The Bluest Eye* shows how Morrison transposes the Black Arts movement's slogan of black is beautiful into a collective effort at racial sublimation aimed at changing racial self-loathing into racial self-love (*Dilution Anxiety* 19). As a result, the dark-skinned black beauty was celebrated and embraced as the epitome of natural beauty (*Dilution Anxiety* 68, 155). Natural beauty became equated with dark-skinned blackness. The advent of the Black Arts movement brought new references to clothing and physical appearances, heralding a new era of self-determination and self-fashioning (*Dilution Anxiety* 68). Appropriation of new clothing, make-up and appearance became part of the performance of black is beautiful (*Dilution Anxiety* 82), just like the new black, Bride, appropriates white clothes and accessories as part of her performance in *God Help the Child*. Owning blackness was part of "the reclamation of racial beauty," which made Morrison think the claim was a necessity (*Dilution Anxiety* 90). The Black Arts movement's sensibility influenced *The Bluest Eye* just as the post-Black Arts movement influenced her later novels like *Song of Solomon*, *Tar Baby*, *Jazz*, and *Paradise* (*Dilution Anxiety* 90). Morrison's latest novel, *God Help the Child*, offers a new take on black is beautiful influenced by the new black ethos with the idea that being black, tar black, midnight black, too black or glassy black is the new norm or novelty.

Historical Act of Passing

Like du Bois, Morrison redefines the twenty-first century's problem of colorism as a struggle to pass. Passing is a narrative of colorism which privileges a life of lighter shades of blackness (*Dilution Anxiety* 65). Crawford defines "colorism" "as a way of distinguishing between the black and white color line and the interracial dynamics of lighter- and darker-skinned blackness" (*Dilution Anxiety* 2); and in the context of black is beautiful movement of the 1960s, it is "overdetermined by both the familiar fetishism of light skin as well as the counter-fetishism of dark skin" (*Dilution Anxiety* 2). *God Help the Child* deals with contemporary issues of racial passing, the crossing of color line, in the context of the new black aesthetics, neatly summed up by the textual expression of "black is the new black." The new black is Morrison's trope of racial passing for the black identity of the new millennium (and its transitions through pre- and post-civil rights to the new millennium). The new black is a culmination of pre-civil rights and post-civil sensibilities. According to Michele Elam, the conventions and politics of passing are being transformed in the twenty-first century (Elam 117–8), so the trope is appropriate for representing the fluid, indeterminate, malleable and shifting nature of all racial identities, especially in a cultural landscape fast becoming increasingly multiracial and multi-ethnic. It represents African Americans' struggle to integrate into mainstream society in order to access full citizenship rights. According to Julie Cary Nerad, the fluid, multicultural body is the ideal medium through which to express the twenty-first century passing narrative, documenting the struggles of African Americans, minorities and the undocumented people (Nerad 13). Thematically, narratives of racial passing dealt with the trials of light-skinned black people who crossed the color line to become assimilated into the more privileged mainstream white society. Ironically, this includes white people who can trace their genealogy to African ancestry. Under the law of hypo-descent or the one-drop rule, such whites or multiracials are default blacks. The novel estimates these passers to be roughly twenty percent (3). However, as Elam observes, racial passing's statistical estimate "bears little on its cultural and literary relevance to the national drama over it" (Elam 99).

The peak years for narratives of passing were from the late 19th century to early 20th century, reportedly passing out in the 1950s (Hobbs 24) and continuing to decline post-1960s (Dreisinger 121), partially due to the collapse of legalized segregation after the advent of the civil rights movement (Hobbs 26). Michele Elam, in her book *The Souls of Mixed Folks*, observes that the decline in narratives of passing was largely because "the ending of legal segregation and the transformations in racial politics of the 1960s made the theme of passing politically irrelevant [. . .]. By the 1970s, discussions of passing were by and large confined to literary studies of passing fiction" (Elam 99–100). However, the passing narrative witnessed a revival of interest in the post-civil rights period. According to Dreisinger, the passing narrative has always thrived during moments of identity crisis and social unease about racial categories (Dreisinger 123). It has resurfaced as a product of anxiety about contemporary racial and ethnic ambiguities, which are fast becoming fluid in an era of hybridity and global cultural exchange (Dreisinger 123). In this era of floating and fluid cultural heritage and identity, everyone seems to be passing for someone else. As Samira Kawash succinctly summarizes, "we are what we are passing for?" (qtd. in Dreisinger 125). Expanding upon Kawash's notion of passing, Dreisinger observes that passing narratives "reflect growing acceptance of the fact that because race is indeed a construct, and racial categories are not as rigid as we once believed them to be, then any racial identity involves passing" (137). This revival of interest in the genre of passing narrative links to Juda Bennett's observation that the genre of passing continued to survive, despite the downturn in the 60s, with renewed interest, especially in the 80s, from the publication of Deborah McDowell's provocative introduction to Nella

Larsen's *Passing* (Bennett "Toni Morrison and the Burden" 206). According to Michele Elam, the theme of passing assumed "a rather spectacular new life" with the publication of millennial novels like Colson Whitehead's *The Institutionist* and Philip Roth's *The Human Stain*. The reader can add to this list of millennial novels of passing Morrison's *God Help the Child*. These novels enable renewed investigation of what it means to be black or non-black and passing as both a form of "social inquiry and literary analysis" (Elam 92). These millennial novels of racial passing challenged the meaning of race and the construction of racial identities at the dawn of this new century.

The theme of passing overlaps with African Americans' struggle for freedom and equal rights and their desire to have a more egalitarian socioeconomic status. *God Help the Child* presents the predicaments of those who passed for white in order to escape the economic and social inequities of racism. The passers wanted to escape the daily humiliations, indignities, experience of racism, violence and all the socioeconomic hardships faced by black and second-class citizens (Nerad *Passing Interest* 46). Many colored people passed for white in order to get better employment and to achieve greater upward mobility (Nerad *Passing Interest* 74). African Americans understood that they could be socially disenfranchised due to the disadvantages of their skin color. They wanted to live a life free from racial discrimination and daily indignities. By passing for whites, they turned their backs on their racial background and families. Their act of passing was often interpreted as a sign of betrayal, racial self-loathing or simply a denial of blackness. For example, Sweetness' grandmother, who passed for white, turned her back on her family. Once she had dissociated herself from her black racial identity, she severed all familial ties, which goes against the African American culture of reaching out to family in need of help (Nerad *Passing Interest* 45). Unconcerned whether her act of passing was considered betrayal or cowardice, once she had crossed the color line, she drew it firmly between herself and her family by returning all the letters from her family members without opening or acknowledging them out of fear of exposure. Passing offered the prospect of a better future but disrupted familial relationships forever. The decision to disavow family can be motivated by cowardice or shame at being identified with people who could be treated worse than animals. Lack of self-respect, and its facile opposite, racial pride, are the main motivations behind the desire to pass or cross the color line (Nerad *Passing Interest* 74). In *God Help the Child*, the characters do so to obtain the legal rights and privileges unavailable to Jim Crow's second-class citizens (Norman "The Dilemma of Narrating Jim Crow" 39).[1]

God Help the Child is Morrison's most contemporary work, and therefore important for the study of racial passing in the context of the post-racial, post-black and new black discourses. This invariably begs the question of what it means to pass as the new black, especially in the context of post-black discourses when skin color is still both transcendent and an obstacle to economic success.[2] The answer lies in how race continues to be an important factor, a determinant in the construction of racial identity, for African Americans. According to Allyson Hobbs, "Passing is continuous and enduring historical phenomenon that opens a wide window onto larger issues about inconstant racial definitions, the changing dynamic of race relations, and the complex and circuitous routes along which African American identity has developed in the United States" (*A Chosen Exile* 24). The theme of passing enables Morrison to question race relations, especially in this so-called post-racial or beyond race era. Morrison's objective and practice of racial passing in *God Help the Child* comes closer to Michele Elam's observation, "The novels of racial passing have risen seemingly from the dead not to bear witness to past issues but to testify in some of the fiercest debates about the viability of race in this 'beyond race' era" (Elam ch. 3). The beyond race era is the so-called overly optimistic era of post-racialism symbolically ushered in with Obama's rise to the presidency, the most powerful head of government in the world. Post-racialism is a misleading expression as it fails to encompass black aspirations and potentialities. Spearheaded and ushered in by figures like Winfrey, Obama and other artists, post-black or the new black would still be a choice word to refer to the 21st century black struggles to *pass* through whiteness to success.

Morrison's novels reflect the flexibility and adaptability of life to societal pressures in various historical eras. Her novels are interconnected with each other through the themes of passing. According to Juda Bennett, Morrison's treatment of the passing myth in her first seven novels and the short story "Recitatif" is brief and oblique ("Toni Morrison and the Burden" 213). For example, Pecola in *The Bluest Eye* cannot physically pass for white, yet she is at one with the desires and aspirations of a passing figure: She "possesses the key emotional characteristics: a desire for white privilege and an increasing disassociation from the black community." According to Bennett, "Morrison presents characters who are capable of physically passing for white, and so the dynamics of crossing the color line are moved from the body to the psyche" ("Toni Morrison and the Burden" 206). Bennett's observation on Pecola's desire for the bluest eye evokes the passing character's desire for whiteness, which can be applied to Bride. Pecola's obsession about the bluest eye is similar to Bride's fascination with whiteness. Bennett quotes other useful examples from the oeuvre of Morrison until the publication of Morrison's short story, "Recitatif." For example, when Milkman in *Song of Solomon* sets out to trace his ancestry in the South, he learns about his family history from Susan Byrd, who reveals that Milkman's relative,

Sing, is typical of a conventional passing figure and remarkably similar to the passing predicament faced by Sweetness and her mother, Lula Mae. Milkman's grandmother was "too dark to pass" but she "started passing like the rest of 'em." She adds: "There used to be a lot of that. A lot of it. Not so much nowadays, but there used to be a lot of 'em did that—if they could" (*Song of Solomon* 290). And those who could not, or did not, because it was shameful, ended up regretting that (4). With the publication of *God Help the Child*, Morrison not only comments upon the continued significance of passing as a historical phenomenon, but also develops it as a literary genre and modern existential paradigm. As racial identities became more indeterminate and malleable, passing as the new black became more viable/plausible. This makes the reader reconsider Bennett's observation on how Morrison conceived and discussed the theme of racial passing in her past novels, and how she gradually became more interested in "actually depicting the character or drama of passing" ("Toni Morrison and the Burden" 210). Highlighting the continued social oppression and victimization of the black body long after slavery was abolished and the advancement in post-civil rights era, Morrison depicts passing as an act of survival.

Passing as an Act of Survival

The acts of passing sum up the desperate measures mothers take in order to protect their children from (physical) harm and abuse. *God Help the Child* opens with Sweetness' monologue "to defend herself from ethical judgment" (Goldberg), as she contemplates the circumstances surrounding the birth of her queer-of-color daughter, Lula Ann Bridewell, also known as Bride, whom she defines as "Midnight black, Sudanese black" (3). It is not till the birth of her child when she realizes that she has been herself passing as light-skinned all her life.[3] The birth of this black baby brings up the history of passing in her family. She contemplates how passing for white offered a medium of survival in a racist society like the US: "Almost all mulatto types and quadroons did that back in the day" (3). Invoking the 19th century nomenclature of mulatto types and quadroons, Morrison plays upon the concept of race as a form of socially-constructed fiction, meaning that "notions of racial difference are human creations rather than eternal, essential categories" (Bonilla-Silva *Racism without Racists* 8). According to Valerie Babb,

> This social dimension of race is illuminated by terms such as quadroon, octoroon, or mestizo which attempt to make distinct from whites those individuals with identical physical appearance but fractions of speciously documentable nonwhite blood. These terms illustrate that, as a

means of human classification, race can ignore shared physical resemblance and categorize on the basis of assigned social legacy.

(Babb 10)

The nomenclature of mulatto types and quadroons represented social and legislative attempts to prevent such people from passing (Elam 3). This effort to contain African Americans from passing is one of the most defining themes in African American literature. It embodies the famous du Boisean problem of the color line, which is still an obstacle to the socioeconomic success of minorities: "The problem of the Twentieth Century is the problem of the colour line" (du Bois). At the dawn of the 21st century, the color line still runs through most daily human interaction. The person who passes for white still confronts the color line and lives a "bifurcated" life. He/She can pass for white in order to survive in a racially segregated society and take advantage of differential economic opportunities or better residential accommodation and education. Many African American women, in particular, passed for white in order to escape slavery and segregation, to attain freedom and promise of a better future for their children (Zackodnick xxvi).

Morrison's passing characters "embody the paradox of race and color" because race is a social construct and not a physical attribute (Pfeifer 2, Dreisinger 123). Even if the characters pass for white or light-skinned, blackness can become their default due to some remote ancestry or genealogy, as is the case with Sweetness. Bride's black baby will expose the family tree which both parents, Sweetness and her husband Louis, are unwilling to acknowledge because it exposes their inherited blackness, before they successfully crossed the color line as fair-skinned blacks, or multiracial, rather than being black. Even a remote trace of black blood exposes Sweetness' fear of blackness, of becoming all of a sudden black and visible, which impacts her aspiration to succeed in America, to "hold on to a little dignity" (4). It was nigh impossible to conceive that a black person could possess a life of dignity. Passing provided the medium through which the passer could reclaim a life of dignity and daily freedoms like trying on a hat as a serious buyer and without being thought a thief. Morrison links the same desire to succeed with the upward mobility associated with passing and the theme of the new black. For example, Sweetness' grandmother passed for white to seize opportunities for an upscaled life. She cut herself off from her black family because contact with black relatives would harm her social standing. Passing, as Kathleen Pfeiffer observes, is "predicated on the secret of one's birth and the renunciation of one's family" (Pfeifer 1). Sweetness' grandmother's act of renouncing her family or black affiliation can be read in the tradition of passing narratives as an act of racial self-hatred or disloyalty (Pfeiffer 2) or an act of survival in a segregated society like the Jim

Crow. She moves away from family members to give her children "a highly pruned version of the family tree" (Mills *Blackness Visible* ch. 3). There is a similar act of passing in Morrison's novel *Jazz*. Golden Gray's mother is white, but his father is black. His mother consciously tries to steep him in white culture. Gray's acculturation becomes successful. As a result, he acts white, becomes white and appears, thinks and behaves white, although after his encounter with Wild and a confrontation with his father, he seems to embrace his blackness. Many white Americans, like Gray, have black ancestry but pass for white. In fact, by the very definition of the one-drop rule, they are actually black, as Sweetness claims to be the case (3).

Passing also reflects du Bois' famous state of "twoness" or "double-consciousness," which Morrison develops into the modern-day metaphor of Oreo or Oreoness—black from outside but white within. An Oreo is a paradigmatic person who identifies himself/herself as white, dissociated from black culture. Oreo captures the split subjectivities, multiple consciousness and the inherent contradictions of the black experience in a white supremacist society. It is Morrison's take on the new black who "fills in 'white' on bureaucratic forms" (Mills *Blackness Visible* ch. 3). It embodies Morrison's designation of the new black who is divided—black on the outside but white within. Bride, as the new black or Oreo, adopts white to be assimilated and succeed as a business entrepreneur. She embraces a virtual courtesy whiteness by passing appropriate "cultural tests" and distinguishing herself from unreconstructed blacks to avoid being mistaken for one by a waiter in a restaurant. The concept of passing, as Juda Bennett points out, helps the author challenge "essentialist metaphors of 'black' and 'white' and helps Morrison deconstruct the romantic myth of beauty that 'the outer face reflects the inner person'" (Bennett *The Passing Figure* 37). Bennett recalls how poets like Mathew Arnold combined metaphors of "sweetness and light," which increasingly changed into "darkness and light" by writers like Poe, Melville and Conrad (Bennett *The Passing Figure* 17), as Morrison avers to be the case in her classic study *Playing in the Dark: Whiteness and the Literary Imagination*. Bride's mother, Sweetness, whose name itself encapsulates the concept of passing—sweetness was associated with being light (colored)—reminisces on how her own mother, Lula Mae, could easily pass for white due to the color of her skin but "chose not to" (3–4). Until the moment of Bride's birth, Sweetness was unconsciously or unintentionally passing for white because from her own account, she is "light-skinned, with good hair, what we call high yellow" (3). High yellow is beautified and desirable in the post-slavery post-Black Arts imagination (Crawford *Dilution Anxiety* 34). This remark reveals the color-struck imagination of Bride's mother. Jean Wyatt describes Sweetness as a colorist mother. She is the victim of an epidermalization complex (in a society which invests or reifies skin); she attaches too much importance to her daughter's skin color and begins to detest her. Perhaps, because she has reified light skin, she is unable to look at or touch that which is "too black." Unlike her mother or father, Lula Ann is tar black and can expose her parents, who can easily pass for a white or light-skinned couple. In fact, Lula Ann becomes a cause of embarrassment for her mother. Sweetness wishes her daughter "hadn't been born with that terrible colour" (5). She even acknowledges that she could have nursed and cared for her daughter if "our skin colors were reversed" (6), rather than having to live with the nightmare of having "a pickaninny sucking at [her] teat" (5).

Fear of the Atavistic Child

In the vein of traditional narratives of passing, such as Langston Hughes' short story "Passing," in which a son is embarrassed to acknowledge his mother in public and walks past ignoring her, in *God Help the Child*, a mother, ashamed of being identified as the mother of a black baby, asks her daughter to call her "Sweetness" not "mother" or "mama," because "too thick-lips calling [her] 'Mama' would confuse people" (6). This is one way Morrison highlights the dangers of internalizing not only white standards of beauty but the racist stereotypes associated with blackness like pickaninnies, mommies, jezebels, coons, Oreos and welfare queens.[4] These stereotypes and stock figures constitute the "racialist symbolic" whose objective is to curtail and deny the subjectivity of black people (Taylor P. *Black is Beautiful* ch. 2). The prevalence of these stereotypes reveals anti-black prejudice and the danger of internalizing them, an obvious source of a black inferiority complex. Again, the mother-daughter relationship in *God Help the Child* is especially reminiscent of the mother-daughter relationship in *The Bluest Eye*. In *The Bluest Eye*, the mother, Pauline, describes her daughter Pecola, at birth, as "a black ball of hair" (122). She valorizes whiteness so much that her own child becomes undesirable: "But I knowed she was ugly. Head full of pretty hair, but Lord she was ugly" (124). Pecola, like Bride, desires her mother's touch as token of love and acceptance, but is also sensitive to her mother's reaction and expressions of love. For example, she remembers how her pretty hair became "tangled black puffs of rough wool to comb" for her mother, who had internalized images of white beauty so much that she started distancing herself from her daughter just as Sweetness did from her daughter, Bride: "Pauline begins to distance herself from her child's body, identifying it as another strike against her own self, since the issue of her body cannot approximate the likes of Shirley Temple" (Yancy *Black Bodies* 195). Sweetness also distances herself from her fear of exposure, of publicly acknowledging Bride as her daughter, a source of shame. Not acknowledging her "throwback" or racially atavistic child—who can reveal the racial traits of previous generations—is to protect her act of passing. She may be afraid to acknowledge her child because of the one-drop rule, which can lead to legal disenfranchisement by revealing the biological or genetic situation of the mother (Elam 13). The racially atavistic child is a common trope in "black baby fables" written by white authors in the late 19th and early 20th century, whose aim was to warn "injudicious white women against the dangers of mates without pedigree" (Nerad *Passing Interest* 106). They offered a word of caution against interracial marriages and sex in the post-civil rights era. According to Jené Schoenfeld, the fiction of atavism plays upon the fear of the violation of racial boundaries and that the "racial difference is real and could reappear in the form of a concrete body whose outside matches" what is perceived to be inside (Schoenfeld 106). This fantasy of atavism was exaggerated so that the public fear of violation could be exploited to construct these very exclusionary boundaries of identity. Thus, the trope of the black baby emerges "as a potential source of exposure for the passer" (Schoenfeld 106).

Black authors of the Harlem Renaissance also produced the black baby as "an important variant in the literary representations" of passing fiction as indicative of racial crisis (Schoenfeld 106). Morrison's act of situating the tale, especially the birth and nurturing difficulties of Lula Ann, in the nineties—the so-called era of neo-liberalism and the peak of the multiracial movement—grapples with the challenging issues of identity crisis. Until Lula Ann's pale birth skin changed her skin to blue-black right in front of her mother, she was not aware of her own unintentional act of passing. She was passing because people did not assume her to be black. Now the blue-black baby is the potential source of exposure for the unpretentious passing mother, through which her pretense to passing could be exposed. If people were to know that she is the biological mother of a black baby, they would know she was black too. With her blackness, Lula Ann could expose her parents' act of passing to the community. Above all, she has *outed* her mother and father (and perhaps ancestors) to each other. Her dark skin will make her parents lose their social status.

Despite the post-civil rights and post-Jim Crow development in race relations, Sweetness finds herself anxious and insecure. Her feelings of insecurity and the need to pass are linked to the lack of a stable home or place in a racist society. She feels so embarrassed and ashamed she even, for a moment, "put blanket over her face" and pressed as preferable to acknowledging Lula Ann as her daughter in public. Lula Ann also complicates and disrupts the relationship between her mother and her father, Louis. She drives a wedge between her parents and breaks their marriage "to pieces" (5). Both fall victim to the skin-color trap (Crawford *Dilution Anxiety* 26) after they argue over how their daughter has inherited the black color of her skin and from whom. Lula Ann's blue-black skin reveals the tell-tale sign of black ancestry (and plays upon the fear of interracial marriage) which each parent is afraid to acknowledge, hence the shock and disbelief over her birth. Afraid of being labeled black, both want to disown part of the identity that healthy race pride or self-regard would make them desire to embrace.

Lack of dignity, healthy self-regard and racial pride were, in addition to socioeconomic motivations behind the decision to cross the color line. The atavistic child embodies the possibility or inescapable reality of "a blood-borne set of traits" that can expose the potential passer's secret genealogy or black ancestry (Schoenfeld "Can One Really Choose?"106). To protect herself from the blame or insinuation that Bride might be the result of an extra-marital relationship, Bride's mother blames her husband or his family, claiming they are responsible for the black color of the daughter. Sweetness' husband leaves her after she tells him that "[Bride's] blackness must be from his own family—not mine" (6). Feeling outraged, Louis leaves Sweetness alone to look after the child. Sweetness resigns herself to the fact that her daughter is black. Her account of Lula Ann's birth is remarkably similar to the way du Bois remembers the circumstances surrounding the birth of his son. She becomes reconciled to the birth of her daughter just as du Bois does to the birth of his son, "Within the veil was he born, said I; and there within shall he live—a Negro and a Negro's son" (*The Souls of Black Folk*).[5] However, as Cornel West observes, du Bois manages to muster "salvific hope" in his characterization of his son's birth and his subsequent tragic death, a symbolic journey of black life in white supremacist America. He reads in his son's sojourn "not the end" but the sign of "some mighty morning to lift the Veil" (West *The Cornel West Reader* 572). West rightly reads some "dose of stoicism" and hope for the future in du Bois' efforts to come to terms with the fate of his son (573).

Sweetness, who has to navigate through the color line still impacted by the new Jim Crow regime, has du Boisean apprehensions about her daughter—linking her very dark blackness to a bleak essentialist future deprived of social mobility—without realizing that the beginning of the twenty-first century, which witnessed considerable progress in race relations, offers new possibilities to a self-fashioning new black millennial like Bride, who embodies the spirit of the new black willing to embrace limitless potentialities. This era, albeit defined by random police brutality, acts of racially motivated violence and murder against the black and other minorities, also witnessed huge black success in all walks of life, spearheaded and symbolized by Obama's success in the White House. Such examples of black success and upward mobility mainly depend upon the ability to claim and manipulate a black racial identity, which Bride does in her successful career as a business entrepreneur. For example, Obama's success was due to his ability to pass and claim an identity that was black, multiracial and transcendent. He did not claim an African American racial kinship because he was not a descendant of slaves. The most influential persons in his life, like his mother and grandparents, had white ancestry. Obama had to appropriate both blackness and whiteness as an act of political expediency, to move ahead by way of performing "a racial balancing act" (Hobbs *A Chosen Exile* 274). Unable to foresee the promise of the new millennium for the millennials like Bride, Sweetness ends the monologue on a note of, to borrow a useful term from David Bradley, "achromatic resignation." Bradley defines achromism as a system of belief "from the Greek a-, meaning 'not', and chroma, meaning 'color'), which is that within the context of the society to which I belong by right—or misfortune—of birth, nothing I shall ever accomplish or discover or earn or inherit or give away—nothing I can ever do—will outweigh the fact of my face in determining my destiny" (qtd. in Martin 38). Like Cain's mark, Lula Ann's blackness will remain a liability—a cross she will have to carry for the rest of her life. This resignation is at odds with the spirit of the new black, as we shall see. Sweetness envisages her daughter in future, like Fanon, as the eternal victim of her essence or appearance for which neither mother nor daughter are responsible. Old or new, Bride will have to play the part of being black and live up to the new racist projections and myths. She will have to negotiate a new regime of racial fetishes, images and stereotypes. In her highly nuanced characterization of Bride, Morrison reshapes the figure of the passer from the old black to the new black to address the contemporary issues of racial identity, mother-daughter relationships and issues of upward mobility: how the act of passing becomes a denial of race and impacts on mother-child relations (Bennett *The Queer Pleasure* 144). Bride will have to adapt to the burden of identities historically offered to blacks. Although she will challenge the racial construction of her identity, she is unable to refute it or liberate herself from the racially imposed construction of her identity as the new black. Again, the real issue is racism and its pernicious impact on the well-being of characters who have to renegotiate their lives when faced with moments of racial interpellation.

Notes

1. According to Kenneth W. Mack and Guy-Uriel E. Charles, the provocative term "the new black" continues to challenge the "continued relevance of civil rights idea as we enter more fully the twenty-first century" ("Introduction" 2).
2. Morrison defines color in terms of pharmakon—"both a curse and a blessing"— in her discussion of *God Help the Child* in *The Origin of Others* (ch. 2).

3. According to Jesse A. Goldberg, Sweetness, just like Sethe, commits violence in her attempt to "exercise maternal ethics." She rightly observes at the start of her essay that it is reductive to view Morrison's characters, especially mothers, from "a single ethical judgment" because of the complex situations she places them in. I think Sweetness faced, to borrow the expression from Jean Wyatt, with the aporetics of motherhood due to (internalised) racism and fear of exposure and public shame as she considers herself outed because the tar-black color of her daughter's skin, exposes the sham of her unpretentious passing for fair-skinned.

4. According to Patricia Hill Collins, stereotypes like the welfare queen constitute a set of "socially constructed controlling images of Black womanhood, each reflecting the dominant group's interest in maintaining Black woman's subordination" (Collins 71). See also Angela Y. Davis' essay "Black Women and Welfare," where she discusses perpetuation of black stereotypes, increased black female poverty and the subsequent dependence upon welfare as a result of Reagan's policies when he took office in 1981.

5. Critics, like Janine Jones, have read a similar and fatalistic reaction to that of Sweetness' over the birth and future of her daughter, in response to the way du Bois comes to terms with the fact that his son was born black and the kind of future life he could inherit as his birth right in a racist society like the United States (Jones 218).

2 Passing as the New Black

> Whether he likes it or not, the black man has to wear the livery the white man has fabricated for him.
>
> (Frantz Fanon)

Guilt and Shame

This part of my discussion is from Bride's perspective. She tells her story after the breakup with her boyfriend, Booker. She uses the liquid metaphor of melting away to describe her sense of dismemberment or loss of subjectivity after her boyfriend abruptly ends their relationship by announcing that she is not the woman he wants. In Bride's eyes, this is a total negation of her personality. She suffers low self-esteem. She thinks she is deficient (although she is the embodiment of a successful self-made woman): "Not pretty enough or exciting" (8). Above all, her boyfriend blames her for being incapable of thinking: "I can't have thoughts of my own?" (8). The breakup scene between Bride and her boyfriend, Booker, is reminiscent of the breakup between Florens and the blacksmith in *A Mercy*. The blacksmith denigrates Florens in a way similar to how Booker treats Bride. When the blacksmith wants to end his relationship with Florens and expel her from his place, he "replicates in all its semantic force, the orthodox conception of the slave—a mere thing without any activity of mind or body—'a sheer wilderness'" (Akhtar 42) by saying: "You are nothing but wilderness. No constraint. No mind" (139). He also accuses her of being irrational, lacking reason: "Your head is empty and your body is wild" (139). The blacksmith reduces Florens' subjectivity to that of being a raced object (Akhtar 42), while Bride's boyfriend draws up an essentialist identity for Bride, which denies her any capacity for rational thinking and ownership of agency or subjectivity.

However, her breakup with Booker does not mean the end of the world for Bride. It does not prevent her from focusing on her business and fulfilling her commitments. She becomes more proactive and decides to pay a

long overdue visit to Sofia Huxley. Huxley was accused of child molesta-
tion and given a prison sentence. Bride was a witness against her to get
closer to her mother, Sweetness, who had been proud when Bride testified against Huxley in order to earn "mother love." Her mother, on the
other hand, wanted Bride to testify to win societal approval and make her
existence more acceptable in a white dominated society (instead of being
looked down upon or scorned), which it did. Thus, desperate to please both
her mother and society to gain social acceptance, Bride had testified against
Huxley. Although "[t]here was lots of other testimony about [Huxley's]
molestations (30)," it was all baseless and without any concrete evidence.
In fact, Huxley was innocent of the crime for which she was wrongly sen-
tenced. Bride, aware of having falsely testified against Huxley, feels guilty
of having done her wrong. This is the hidden source of her shame she feels
the need to redress.

As I noted earlier in my study of Morrison, guilt and shame are two hidden agents of subjectivity behind some of Morrison's recent characters
like Frank Money in *Home* (Akhtar 134–8).[1] There are two experiences
of shame suffered by both mother and daughter in *God Help the Child*.
Sweetness is acutely conscious of and experiences external shame—of the
spectatorial or judgmental gaze of others who make her feel ashamed, as
the mother of a daughter she feels ashamed to acknowledge as her own.
Bride, on the other hand, experiences internal guilt, which makes her take
ethical account of her decision making (in the past and present) to redress
her wrongdoing. Both mother and daughter suffer the negative impact of
what bell hooks defines as "racialised shaming," which can result from
standards of acceptance, beauty and forms of verbal or physical attack.
Hooks considers these as "central component[s] of racial assault" (qtd. in
Stockton *Beautiful Bottom* 9). Most of Morrison's characters, like Frank
Money, are unable to organize themselves and their relations with others
meaningfully unless they can come to terms with their internalized guilt.
After her breakup, Bride experiences shame induced by her exposure to
guilt. The source of this shame comes not from individual actions as such,
but from membership of a community implicated in these kinds of deeds
(Tillet *Sites of Slavery* 91). She recognizes her responsibility for destroy-
ing Huxley's life. To make amends, to help Sofia "get a good start" on her
life outside prison, Bride prepares a "gift package of You, Girl," and "two
envelopes—the slim one with the airline gift then the fat one with five thousand dollars. About two hundred dollars for each year if she served her full
sentence" (20). This was her way of fulfilling a promise to herself to do a
"good Samaritan" turn, which backfires unexpectedly. Upon realizing Lula
Ann Bridewell, Bride, is "one of the children who" stood witness against
her, she gives Bride the hammering of her life.

As Bride tries to recover from Sofia's attack, she contemplates: "Nothing announced her attack on me. I'll never forget it, and even if I tried to, the scars, let alone the shame, wouldn't let me" (29). The severe physical scars she talks about are also the wounds of her shame. She finds memory the worst part of healing (21). She remembers how dependent she was upon her mother and how she yearned for her love and attention. Above all, she wanted her mother to hold her so that she could feel her touch. Touch in Morrison's fiction is a medium of subjectivity.[2] It restores self-image and lays the foundation of human relationship and makes the mother-daughter bond stronger and trustworthy. Bride always knew that her mother did not like touching her: "I used to pray she would slap my face or spank me just to feel her touch. I made little mistakes deliberately, but she had ways to punish me without touching the skin she hated" (31). Fearing maternal reprisals, she felt insecure. Fear and obedience were "the only survival choice" (32). She became compliant and to make her mother proud, she testified against Sofia Huxley: "Brilliantly, I know, because after the trial Sweetness was kind of motherlike" (32).

Clothing the New Black

After Bride becomes the object of Huxley's assault, she reverts to her old self and becomes: "Lula Ann who never fought back. Ever" (32). She looks at her black-and-blue face in the mirror and remembers Jeri's advice on how to make sure blackness sells. She consulted him in order to manage her self-image and advance her career. He even advised Bride how to choose her accessories and make-up carefully. According to Jeri, Bride should wear only white pearl jewelery. It is the white female signifiers, like jewelery and other accessories, which heighten the contrast when worn by the black body. As Lisa B. Thompson observes with reference to Condoleezza Rice and her choice of carefully selected pearl jewelery, "Many white women also wear these items, but it is the presence of a black female body that changes how they signify and resonate" (Thompson L. 7). Jeri's imperative of white only renders Bride one-dimensional. By making Bride wear white only, Jeri wants to redefine her personality, to enact her difference by enhancing her blackness. By accentuating her blackness and bodily features, he makes Bride hypervisible and exposes Bride's attempt at passing and hence her race. In order to access mobility, prestige, safety and status, African Americans had to wear certain styles of clothing and footwear. From history, we learn that African American women who wanted to dress like ladies, especially with white accoutrements "were viciously attacked by those who aimed to keep them in their place and thus on the outside of respectable society" (Willet "Trayvon Martin"). Traditionally, white dresses symbolize femininity, innocence, sexual purity or virginity (associated with white women). All these ideals evoke puritanical and Victorian values.³ However, white's appropriation by a non-white like Bride, to enhance her sexual appeal and desirability or eroticization, reveals the inverse side of white clothes when worn by a black woman. Instead of being symbolic of their innocence, of literally being brides (consider the author's intended pun on the name Bride, also reminiscent of the new "brides" of pop culture like Britney Spears, Christina Aguilera and Beyoncé (Hobson *Body as Evidence* 53), white clothes on black women reveal the sexual nature of black women hidden under their white clothes (Ziegler "Black Sissy Masculinity"). Even African Americans, including veterans, who "unintentionally inverted social norms by embracing the social norms of respectability [. . .] often paid a tragic price" (Willet "Trayvon Martin"). For example, the zootsuitors, who haunt Morrison's character Frank in *Home* in the shape of spooky specters, were seen as "race rebels." A latter day reincarnation, as in the case of Trayvon Martin and other rebel youth, is associated with the hoodie-wearing generation, with the hoodie itself becoming a signifier of guilt and suspicion of those who hang around and do nothing. So far, the hoodie has not become symbolic of protest against a white power structure. According to Crawford, it became "an icon of young black men's lack of protection against police brutality" after the killing of Trayvon Martin (*Black Post-Blackness* ch. 1).

Jeri is an image-maker. He induces Bride to discipline her life according to the strict measures of the white code and white imaginary. Bride's compliance with Jeri's imperative white only makes her a martyr to clothes, a slave of colorism, which Morrison describes as the enslavement of senses and appearances. Draping Bride's body in white only heightens the contrast between whiteness and blackness. It overdetermines her blackness against the fetishism of whiteness (Crawford *Dilution Anxiety* 4). Whiteness serves as "the chromatic default," which heightens the racialized contrast and features of Bride's jet-black body (Fleetwood *On Racial Icons* 63). Bride's chromatic and hypervisible blackness recalls Jadine, in *Tar Baby* being taken aback by the tar-black beauty of a woman wearing a "long canary yellow dress" in the market (45). Jadine finds herself "transfixed" by her beauty like everybody else in the store (45). She wonders if she is fascinated by the woman because of her height or the contrast between "the skin like tar against the canary yellow dress?" (45). Margo Natalie Crawford refers to this scene when Jadine, an aspiring young successful model and entrepreneur like Bride, feels like "fall[ing] in love" with this black woman in yellow's "unphotographable beauty" (*Dilution Anxiety* 98). Jadine finds herself "always ready for another canary-yellow dress, other tar-baby fingers holding three white eggs" (46). Crawford sums up the bedeviled and enrapt fascination Jadine has for the "woman in yellow" as envy of her "tar" black skin which seems to exercise "such a dazzling effect" (*Dilution Anxiety* 98) as does the blue-black skin of Bride and Grace Jones "against the colour white." According to Crawford, such fascination "is embedded in any desire of the exotic" (*Dilution Anxiety* 98). Similarly, by Oreo-eroticizing Bride and making her hypervisible, Jeri not only creates colorist hierarchies but wants to stage her difference through her clothing and reification of whiteness. According to Fleetwood, "Colorist hierarchies depend on a mythic conception of whiteness as the standard of measurement and a totalising blackness as its depraved opposite" (Fleetwood *Troubling Vision* ch. 2). Asking Bride to only wear white reveals Jeri's desire to bleach her black body by draping it in white or putting on an add-on white skin. Clothing, especially white clothing in the present case, is nothing more than a "fabricated, secondary skin" (Stockton *Beautiful Bottom* 44). Its root is the old English word *clitha*, meaning "a poultice," applied to sooth the skin as a protection again sores or inflammation (Stockton *Beautiful Bottom* 43). Jeri assumes the authority to know what best suits the black body of Bride. He calls himself a "total person," which shows that he has the total power to decide her image. As her design consultant, he insists Bride display her black body by exhibiting it dressed all in white (33).

As a cultural agent, Jeri reconstructs the black body of Bride as an image striped black-and-white, a new style or cultural symbol evocative of very dark-skinned black female characters like Jadine from *Tar Baby* and superstars like Grace Jones, whose appearance was fluid and quite often bordered on the androgynous (*Dilution Anxiety* 1). By projecting the permanent norm of whiteness, he highlights the racial markers of her difference. White attire on a black body also affirms contemporary notions of female beauty and the appeal it carries.[4] As bell hooks observes with reference to black fashion celebrities, like Iman, who shine in white on the cover pages of fashion magazines, like Vogue, "when flesh is exposed in attire that is meant to evoke sexual desirability it is worn by a non-white model" (*Black Looks* 72). In other words, expressions of exotic beauty are always inscripted and enhanced when projected on the black female body (Thompson B. 20). Falling victim to sexist/racist mythology, the black model like Iman becomes "the embodiment of the best of the black female savage tampered by those elements of whiteness that soften the image, giving it an aura of virtue and innocence. In the racialized pornographic imagination, she is the perfect combination of virgin and whore, the ultimate vamp" (hooks *Black Looks* 72). According to hooks, "Postmodern notions that black female sexuality is constructed, not innate or inherent, are personified by the career of Iman" (*Black Looks* 72). The character/career of Bride, too, embodies similar notions of postmodern or the new black identity. Read her as you will, new forms and meanings of black identity are born in her character.

New Black and the Forerunners

Jeri's decision to portray Bride as the new black is compatible with the representations of famous black female women and their bodies in a male dominated society. Presenting these women as exotic animals reinforces the image of black exoticism, which feeds into Western cultural imaginary (Thompson B. 29); starting from the earliest example of the Black Venus and her relationship with her handlers like S. Reaux, who presented her black body to Europe as an "animal exhibitor," to that of Baker and Grace Jones. For example, Lisa E. Farrington observes that Josephine Baker's meteoric rise to fame fed the white fantasy of indulging in primitive libidinal desire when Baker performed—in New York and Paris—some of her famous enactments in "Chocolate Dandies, La Revue Negre, and the Folies Bergere" (*Creating Their Own Image* 73). In her French performances, Baker was topless and wore little more than her infamous "banana skirt." Acutely aware of her role as the personification of white fantasies about the primordial nature of blacks—particularly the myth of black female sexuality—Baker's performance included being "carried upside down, like a wounded gazelle, on the back of a robust Martiniquan dancer" to the delight of a frenzied white audience (Farrington 80). According to Farrington, Jones' "approximation of pop culture carnality and androgyny ideally personified the fabled Jezebel, and hip-hop artists such as Foxy Brown and Li'l Kim, whose near-nude and suggestive poses on albums and in publicity photos tested the limits of propriety" (*Creating Their Own Image* 20).

Models and performers, like Grace Jones, adopted certain types of preferred body images and enacted their bodily performances according to these images. According to Katya Foreman, Jones is "a genuine force of nature" ("Grace Jones"). She further observes that in order to expose her "in-your-face sexuality," she "has always sought to further enhance her already powerful physicality through carefully chosen accessories" ("Grace Jones"). According to Foreman, Jones is "the spiritual godmother" of performer singers like Rihanna and Lady Gaga, as she is in the case of Morrison's fictive, Bride, who is urged to enhance her physical appeal by her design consultant, Jeri. Foreman credits Jones for having "rocked a startling outfit or two in her time," courtesy of her handler and once-time partner Jean-Paul Goude, who was captivated by "Jones' raw, prowling grace," and was responsible for projecting "the most powerful images of the singer" ("Grace Jones"). Amongst Jones' performances was the famous show-stealer "at New York Hammerstein Ballroom in 2009" ("Grace Jones").

Here Jones made a stunning appearance in a white headdress and "a white zebra-like tribal bodysuit" ("Grace Jones"). In fact, the white costume outlined her black body and enhanced the exotic appeal of her beauty. Looking at the body of Jones striped in white from the perspective of Jeri and its projection on Bride, it enhanced her exotic sexual appeal and potential or in textual terms, her Oreoness, as it does for Bride.

There are affinities between Goude and Jeri in the way they acted as image-makers and how both Bride and Jones infamously demonstrated their bodies/sexuality according to these men's projected images.[5] Both Goude and Jeri creatively deployed strategies to enhance the racial difference of their subjects developing them into racial icons (Fleetwood *On Racial Icons* 57). Both image-makers reduced these women to objects. Goude confessed that he "was more interested in the virtual character than the real woman" (Foremam). Jeri too aimed at enhancing the virtual character of Bride. He invested her body with images of racial excess and made her the object of his fantasy. He wanted to control and manipulate her image. As a handler, he wants to aestheticize and exaggerate Bride's blackness by enhancing her racialized eroticism. Like Goude, he is vulnerable to the exoticism of Bride's blue-black body. His relationship with Bride exposes the fallacy of post-racialism as he continues to exoticize her body through animal images and makes her body/sexuality an object of desire which is deliciously edible or consumable. Jeri's vocabulary stems from confectionery and zoology. For example, Jeri compares Bride's black body to bonbons, which is a pun. Bonbon is a near anagram of bonobos—a primate most often associated with blacks and their sexuality—the popular conception of inordinate black (female) sexuality as lascivious and animalistic (Peterson *Bestial Traces* 6).

Obviously, the historicity of comparing blacks to apes and simians was to justify their commodification, enslavement and other hierarchies. To use a Fanonian expression, Jeri drapes Bride's black body in "a historico-racial schema" which forces "a racial epidermal schema" upon her (Fanon 84). The historico-racial or zoological schema is woven "out of a thousand details, anecdotes, stories" which make the reader and Bride aware "that there were legends, stories, histories, and above all *historicity*" (Fanon 84). The modern day racist iconography of blacks is made up of all these elements and historicity. Paul C. Taylor points out some of the "depersonalising treatments of blackness" and their representations in the arts and visual culture, calling them "objectifying aesthetic strategies," which operate on two levels: on the level of digests or iconography and on the level of narration or iconology (Taylor P. *Black is Beautiful* ch. 2). The iconographic level is a dialectical relationship between the subject of representation and his\her handler who constructs his\her subjectivity using an "assortment of racial themes that exist in cultural archives and repertoires" (Taylor P. *Black is Beautiful* ch. 2). The subject thus constructed is a matter of iconography and its representation (Jeri will classify Bride according to iconography and its incumbent coding). The handler is conscious of the tensions that exist in the construction of racial iconicity, which vacillate like a pendulum between sublimation and denigration (Fleetwood *On Racial Icons* 66). Taylor claims the motivation behind such iconography may be: How can I suppress or caricature the subject's personality by immersing him/her in racial themes/iconography based on stereotypes and stock images? Or how could I recreate the subject so that the racial images play in the background to capitalize the subject through such a representation? The second level, an extension of the first, concerns "the real-world conditions and consequences of constructing a representation in one way rather than another" (Taylor P. *Black is Beautiful* ch. 2). Here, the hypothetical response to the construction of the subject could consider how the character adds to the repertoire of representations or the kind of real-world work that is achievable. The level of iconology involves stereotypes, caricatures and stock figures which reduce the subjectivity of black people by making them invisible or hypervisible and hypersexual. Stereotypes like "mulatto types," "quadroons," coons, pickaninnies, Oreos, welfare queens, Topsy, Samba or ooga booga, reflect "features that modern racialism conventionally links to blackness" (Taylor P. *Black is Beautiful* ch. 2). They build upon "archetypal personifications of anti-black prejudices" whose aim is to highlight black inferiority and sexuality (Taylor P. *Black is Beautiful* ch. 2).

New Black and the Stereotypes

Like Jeri, Bride's assistant, Brooklyn, also indulges in the racialized construction of the exotic. Both use names, stereotypes and animal imagery, which are common, recognizable and steeped in racist archetypes. These images are more subtle and veiled, but they are the "controlling images" of the post-racial dominant discourse which not only distorts the lived reality of anti-black violence but also its present mode of articulation and significance (Frankowski 12). These images make the viewer incapable of seeing past the skin. Perhaps the point Morrison is making is similar to one made by Patricia Hill Collins about the need to eliminate the "controlling images" embedded in white imaginary in order to combat institutional racism. In *The Origin of Others*, Morrison highlights the power of image to "rule the realm of shaping, sometimes becoming, often contaminating knowledge" (ch. 2). She calls her effort to control the contaminating influence of images "the human project—which is to remain human and to block the dehumanization and estrangement of others" (ch. 2). The stereotypes of black people add to this process of dehumanization. They are embedded in Western culture and give insights into modern day race-thinking. The construction of the racial other as an exotic animal continues to perpetuate stereotypical representation. Colored folks "have been the objects of representation rather than its subjects and creators because racism often determines who gets access to the means of representation in the first place . . . the question of power at issue in the ability to make and wield representations" (Childs *Fade to Black* 16). Therefore, the question of black women's bodies and what they represent is steeped in racial stereotypes. This is especially true considering the rise of the black celebrity, like Josephine Baker, Ross and Jones, as racial icons, whose bodies and performances are associated with racialized sexuality (Fleetwood *On Racial Icons* 71). For example, Baker's widespread popularity is attributed to her exotic appearance with a cheetah and nudity as her costume. The connection between Baker (because of the animal imagery) and other black models of beauty like Ross and Jones (because of white costumes) are clear, as will be seen.

One of Grace Jones' more outrageous performances was appearing as "an animal in a cage," in a performance art designed by her French ex-husband, artist Jean-Paul Goude (Hobson *Venus in the Dark* 97). Jones' performance in the cage created a sense of extreme pastiche in its stereotypical links between black female bodies and bestiality (Hobson *Venus in the Dark* 97–8). According to Janell Hobson, presenting Jones as a powerful tiger would have appeared subversive, were it not for that long tradition of visually representing black people as animals (98). She further observed that "black female sexuality is rendered with the power and allure of a tiger, perhaps alluding to what art critic Miriam Kershaw calls the 'power iconography [of tigers and leopards] among the royalty in certain parts of Africa prior to and during European trade and colonialism'" (98). Jeri utilizes the black female body of Bride to create racial and sexual myths, in much the same way as his predecessors, like Goude and Paul Colin, did. Instead of investing Bride with animal imagery, he should have worked, as Angela Harris argues, to dis-image or dismantle the "opposition between [. . .] animal and African" in order to promote a humanist "politics of respectability" (qtd. in Peterson 7).

Black women as wild and ferocious animals reinforce the myths of black women's sexual savagery and the essential nature of their sensuality, as popularly portrayed by Baker, Ross, Jones and Bride. It renders black female sexuality as bizarre, deviant and grotesque, especially in comparison to white women or white standards of normative beauty and sexuality. Black women are the antithesis of the Western ideal of beauty and womanhood. Historically, the black bodies were gazed upon, examined and assessed on the auction blocks like animals (Yancy *Black Bodies* 114). The figure of Sarah Baartman, also known as the Black Venus or the Hottentot, serves as the prototype and "constitutes a white epistemic orientation to the Black (female) body" (Yancy *Black Bodies* 92). She is one of the earliest examples of the dialectical relationship between whiteness (as pure, good, innocent) compared to Blackness (as impure, bad, freakish, guilty)" (Yancy *Black Bodies* 94). In the opinion of Yancy, "she is the exotic phantasm of white imaginary" (Yancy *Black Bodies* 92). Her body (with its large buttocks) became a site of "a vast operation of distortion and discursive and nondiscursive disciplinary power" (92).

Bride echoes the experiences of Sarah Baartman in her willingness to commodify and display her body according to the advice of her handler, Jeri. Interestingly enough, Jeri appropriated Bride's body as the figure of Galatea (she who is milk white) long before Booker appreciated her beauty as his Galatea. Like the eponymous character Sarah in Andrea Lee's novel *Sarah Phillips*, who plays a game called Galatea in which she stands "naked on a wooden box and turn[s] slowly to have [her] body appraised and criticized," Bride, too, surrenders herself to her Pygmalion—the misogynist Jeri, who shows what other women lack in comparison to Bride (Thompson L. 132). According to Lisa Thompson, "The unimpeachable loveliness of Galatea, so integral to the myth, falls apart when applied to a black female figure" (Thompson L. 132). This happens when the black body is seen through the objectifying gaze, thus rendering the subject far from being an ideal maiden (Thompson L. 132). Bride's performance as Galatea, the artist's object, evokes the archetypal Baartman and other precursors like Baker and Jones vis-à-vis the complicated set of exchanges with their handlers. The commodification of Bride's black body allies her with the objectification of her predecessors like Sarah, Baker and Jones in how they became objects of amusement for white men or their handlers. They all became fascinating objects of sexuality. The history of the black female body has always verged on the exotic, or a racialized construction of exotic sexuality. The black body is an object of curiosity and contradictory forces. Simultaneously repulsive and attractive, Sarah became an object of sexual interest and was socially downgraded. Within the white European imaginary, the black female body, and that of Sarah in particular, was invented "to foreclose any possibility of knowing black women other than as prostitutes" and as sexually deviant (Yancy *White on White* 252). According to Christopher Peterson and George Yancy, this speaks volumes about the eighteenth and nineteenth century discourses and the white male hegemony over black bodies, especially in the late nineteenth century, which constructed female sexuality as pathological in general, and whereby black women "could easily be "seen" as possessing the bestial characteristics of the Black female Hottentot" (Peterson 30, Yancy 94). The most popular example is Sarah, whose body was exhibited like an animal, as an object of curiosity and freak sexuality. Again, there are similarities between Sarah's handler and Jeri. Sarah's handler was "a showman of wild animals named Reaux," who exhibited Sarah in a way that highlighted and sexually exploited her ethnic characteristics. He reduced Sarah to the status of a wild animal (Yancy *Black Bodies* 96). Sarah also became an object of scientific fascination for the prominent French naturalist Georges Curvier, who compared Sarah to exotic animals like the orangutan and the ape in order to highlight "the bestial nature of black women" (Yancy *Black Bodies* 98). She became the measure through which whiteness could define itself (as a symbol of beauty, purity and moral superiority) against blackness (as immoral and sexually lascivious) (Yancy *Black Bodies* 93).

Jeri, too, is a sort of animal exhibitor. Jeri's Oreo-exoticization of Bride's black body in terms of animal imagery evokes historical representation of black women as animal-like (because of their sexual promiscuity) (Yancy *What White Looks Like* 114). His racial animus cannot exoticize Bride's black body without scripting it as an exotic animal, bestial and sexually promiscuous in comparison to white women and women of fair complexion (Yancy *What White Looks Like* 114). Contemporary racism is a clever subterfuge and hides itself behind smokescreens in the garb of backhanded compliments. Given the opportunity, it comes to the surface and expresses itself in distasteful, insulting and racially loaded analogies and vocabulary at both conscious and unconscious levels. Even Bride's assistant, the only person in the world whom she can trust, compares Bride's beaten black-and-blue face to that of an ugly orangutan, drawing upon the racist equation of blacks with apes (Peterson *Bestial Traces* 31): "Worse than anything is her nose—nostril wide as orangutan's" (26). The grown-up Brooklyn behaves like that girl or those boys from her school days who heaped a bunch of bananas on Bride's desk "and did their monkey imitations" (56). This is how Morrison critiques acquired, learned or institutionalized racism, which grown-ups are not able to unlearn.

Comparing black women with white women highlights the binary opposition between blackness and whiteness Morrison demonstrated in *Playing in the Dark: Whiteness and the Literary Imagination*. She characterizes this in the relationship between Jeri and Bride. Jeri's treatment of Bride's black body reduces her to an essentialized representation. She is projected as more lewd and sexual than her white counterparts, who would have to strip naked for the same sex appeal that Bride carries. To strip naked is to denude, to unclothe and appear as exposed and shameless. The representation of the black body as nude has always been featured in the Western arena, and the black female bodies have always served as "potent counterpoints to Western ideologies of white female beauty, womanhood, morality, and civilization"

(Thompson B. 27). As Hortense Spellers has pointed out, the black female body as a comparison is central to the deification of the white woman who embodies the traditional notions of female purity attached to white or fairer skin (qtd. in Zackodnik 107). In comparison to the black body of Bride, white women, the legitimate emblems of beauty in white dominant culture, are perceived as less obscene and sexual. Envious of Bride's financial power and success, their lack of (sex) appeal means, according to Jeri's misogynistic logic, they would have to strip naked to get attention, to claim their power that has been threatened or lost.

Historically, whiteness has been the norm of beauty and the black female body is produced "in excess of idealized white female femininity" (Fleetwood *Troubling Vision* ch. 3). As the new black, Bride inverts the myth of normative white beauty by enhancing "the racial markers of her difference" and producing cross-racial desire and envy amongst women of white and fairer complexion. As the flourishing body, Bride disrupts and threatens "the boundaries for normative codes of the white female body and femininity" (Fleetwood *Troubling Vision* ch. 3). The success of women, like Baker and Bride, "indicates a significant shift in attitude toward the primitive versus the civilized and a new appreciation for things 'wild' and 'libidinous'—qualities still associated with "exotic" black bodies viewed this time with admiration while still maintaining an air of mockery" (Hobson *Venus in the Dark* 95). Acts of wild abandon, which whites believe black bodies can perform better, are associated with celebrating the exotic primitive (Hobson *Venus in the Dark* 95), exemplified in the interactions with their handlers—Baker's with Paul Colin's, Jones' with Goude's, Jeri's with Bride, all of whom reduce the bodies of these models to stereotypes. Comparing black women to wild animals by their handlers involves a way of objectifying their bodies through absolute animal idealization on the one hand, and absolute feminization on the other hand. All these handlers, to use Morrison's expression from *Tar Baby*, are perverse "purveyors of exotics." In Jeri's case, his culturally voyeuristic gaze actually enjoys debasing women by stripping them naked, just like the pedophile who derives sexual gratification by visualizing children as the objects of his fantasy.

Alice Hall observes that Morrison defines the ideal of beauty in terms of a hierarchized relationship between the definers and the defined, based upon exclusion (Hall 54). To extend this argument we can add between the handlers and their subjects, as the case of Goude and Grace, Jeri and Bride. It is important to identify the gazer, the definer, the colonizer and the speaker in order to extend beyond the colonial context or enterprise. According to Iyanla Vanzant, America has not embraced the ideal of black is beautiful in its entirety: "Women of all races [. . .] are programmed to please men. And men control the images that we see [. . .]. He made those things in terms of what is and what is not beautiful. Added to that, black women have to remember that these men are mostly white, coming from a European perspective on what to idealise" (Vanzant 239–40). Jeri wants to visually display Bride's body in a way that enhances her Oreoness. His encounters with Bride can be understood from the perspective of Son in *Tar Baby*, who believes that African Americans are "Appropriated, marketed and trivialised into decor" (129). He also sees in the persona of Alma Estee, wearing the red wig, a series of grotesque and surreal images which appropriate her blackness: "Her sweet face, her midnight skin mocked and destroyed by the pile of synthetic dried blood on her head [. . .] like a bougainvillea in a girdle, like a baby jaguar with lipstick on, like an avocado with earrings" (231). Jeri wants to enhance the exotic appeal of Bride's "licorice skin," because "black is the new black" (33). Jeri's formula for the new black is an extension of the wonderfully surrealist claim "black is beautiful." According to Crawford, Morrison's novels like *The Bluest Eye*, *Tar Baby* (and *God Help the Child*) are part of Morrison's post-Black Arts movement vision, which recognizes that "when black authenticity is no longer written on dark-skinned blackness and hybridity no longer written on light-skinned blackness, it might be possible to reclaim "very blue eyes in a very dark skin," a red wig against "midnight skin" (*Dilution Anxiety* 111) or a yellow or white dress against blue black skin as an experience of surreal beauty that is black. Like the new black, Jadine, in *Tar Baby* who confesses to Valerian that "Picasso *is* better than an Itumba mask" (64), Bride willingly lets Jeri appropriate her blackness. She lets Jeri objectify her body as the new black knowing the implications for her choices and decisions. With little concern for how Jeri's racial fetishism wants to exoticize her body with the visual signs of white-only clothes and accessories, Bride embraces her Oreo identity as part of the surreal beauty of the new black.

Notes

1. See also J. Brooks Bouson's classic *Quiet as It's Kept: Shame, Trauma, and Race in the Novels of Toni Morrison* for an in-depth discussion of aspects of shame in Morrison from *The Bluest Eye* to the publication of *Paradise*.
2. For a full-fledged study of some aspects of touch in Morrison's fiction, especially in *Jazz*, see my discussion in chapter two, "Transgenerational Hauntings and the Magic of Touch in *Jazz*" (Akhtar 71–8). I discuss *Jazz* as a gesture of violence or of restorative self-image and subjectivity with some help from Irigaray's poetics of touch. Katherine Stern also discusses the importance of the tactile over the visual in her interesting essay "Toni Morrison and the Beauty Formula" in Marc C. Conner's *The Aesthetics of Toni Morrison*. She concludes that Morrison's aesthetics of touch is reciprocal, based on the concept of mutual respect, which makes it a liberating gesture.

3. The reader can find plenty of examples in canonical novels like *The Great Gatsby*, *Wide Sargasso Sea* and *The Bell Jar* in which the white female protagonists wear white clothes to indicate their chastity, femininity, virginity and innocence. These white dresses also reflect puritanical and Victorian values.

4. According to Lisa B. Thompson, the selection of white-only accessories by black ladies like Condoleezza Rice present "a challenge to the dominant representation of black womanhood in the public imagination, where one-dimensional images of them as promiscuous, seductive, and sexually irresponsible circulate" (7). Bride's embrace of well-chosen white accessories connects her with the performance of such black womanhood. It especially engages her in conversation with iconic black fashion celebrities like Iman. For me, her white-only appearance particularly links her to Grace Jones' multiple performances wearing white-only accessories. Bride's black body has the same dazzling effect as that of Jones' contrasted with white.

5. The kind of interest Jeri takes in Bride's black body is similar to Goude's in Jones' body. According to Goude, "The strength of [Jones'] image, then as now, is that it swings from the near grotesque—from the organ grinder's monkey—to the great African beauty. You are constantly looking at her and wondering if she's beautiful or grotesque, or both and how can she be one if she is the other" (qtd. in Crawford *Dilution Anxiety* 98).

3   Oreotizing the New Black

> The urgency of distinguishing between those who belong to the human race
> and those who are decidedly non-human is so powerful the spotlight turns
> away and shines not on the object of degradation but on its creator.
>
> (Toni Morrison, *The Origin of Others*)

The New Black Aesthetics

Jeri's formulation of "black is the new black" is a case a study of a new form
of evolutionary racism. In an era of post-racial and post-black/new black
(radicalized) ideology, old "forms of overt racism are no longer socially and
scientifically acceptable"; therefore, "racism has changed from an overt to
an often covert and unconscious form" (Shavers 91). This also entails how
we adapt and respond to this new, covert form of racism. And this partly
embodies what it means to be the new black now. Morrison exposes and
rectifies a mind-set prone to identify black as a racial marker, a biological trait or a cultural construct. Like Rone Shavers, who cautions against
hidden and covert racism, Morrison, too, seems to caution that it does not
matter whether Jeri advocates the new black or not; the fact that Bride possesses "the biological markers for Black will engender racist assumptions,
however casual, naïve or downright hostile" (Shavers 89).

Morrison's concept of the new black embodies a more expansive notion
of black performance and identity, of multifaceted and shapeshifting blackness. It brings up a whole range of aesthetics on black embodiment, post-
blackness and the new black. From Fanon's famous black is always black
(because it is always visible) to black is beautiful, Jeri's new black is subtle,
nuanced, racially loaded and enigmatic. On the face of it, he advises Bride
how to wield and lionize her blackness to her advantage for the job market
and business and helps Bride launch a successful career as an entrepreneur.
He capitalizes on her difference with a series of white-on-black images
aimed at enhancing and exoticizing her blackness or Oreoness, seeing Bride

as an object of commercial value and economic utility. His subject position as her designer makes him the arbiter of her blackness as he successfully advises her how to sell it. His subject position also betrays his racial inclinations and identity. White men take the position of authority, especially in looking relations, i.e., the gazer and the gazed, the looker and the looked-at, the definer and the defined, the colonizer and the colonized, the master and the slave. Under the matrix of these power relations of race and the subject and object positions, the operative behind the dominant cultural gaze is discerned as a figure of white male authority. The fact that Jeri occupies a position of power to control and determine Bride's public appearances and how she appears to herself sums up the Fanonian splits, ruptures of black consciousness and the lived reality of black experience, which are characteristic of racial domination and black subjugation. This is obvious from Jeri's effort to relegate Bride to the level of exoticism to the degree that she loses her sense of racial identity and subjectivity. She becomes the victim of Jeri's mastering and racist gaze. According to George Yancy, whites have always enjoyed the privileges of the gazer and all the power it brings, especially in the context of white racist societies (*Black Bodies* xviii).

Jeri aims at marketing the black body by enhancing its Oreoness and producing it as an object of exotic appeal. His dicta of white-only accessories have less to do with Bride's appearance and more to do with her race and gender. The black body is strictly subject to the imposition of white values or choices in dress code or appearance, totally subordinated to the choices if not prejudices of the "total person," the ultimate authority on dress code and external appearance. Bride becomes Oreo because she recognizes that Jeri has the authority and power to enforce this categorization. Bride's acceptance of her racial identity as Oreo and how she molds her personality and even sexual identity takes place under the pressure of her desire to succeed in her social life. She is not able to question this imposition of identity because she wants to have greater social mobility. The metaphor of Oreo as the passing figure reveals the dynamics of race, how it operates from without and how it is experienced from within. Bride's embrace of whiteness and act of passing as Oreo reveals that the essence of her identity as a successful entrepreneur or the new black resides not in her individual qualities, but in the way she recognizes herself and is recognized by Jeri (and those who interview her for jobs) as playing white.

Jeri's formulation of black as the new black sums up the evolutionary process of being black throughout the ages and carries the load of historical representations of being black and its gendered legacy. Clothes were part of the performance of black is beautiful (Crawford *Dilution Anxiety* 68, 82), to enhance natural black beauty. In Bride's case, white-only clothes operate as "debasement aesthetics" or Oreo-aesthetics (Stockton 64). In creating her identity through white accessories, dress and habits, which threaten her innate subjectivity, Bride becomes an Oreo, which is at one with the stereotyping gaze. Oreo has become a metaphor of the new black, just like drag and spectacle was part of the performance of "Black is Beautiful" (Crawford *Dilution Anxiety* 82). Conscious of her racial alterity/difference, she enacts and lives the racialized imagery and willingly performs her Oreo-eroticized blackness, confirming her racial affiliation in the eyes of her interlocutor, Jeri. Jeri's barrage of white-on-black imagery, which reduces her race to visible difference in skin color, culminates in the trope of a black and white animal, the"panther in snow" (34, 50). It is impossible not to find racial stereotypes or prejudices in his compliments. Morrison, like Fleetwood, points out that the characterization of blackness or the rise of the new black associated with black celebrities or racial icons "tends to be read within a representational space of negation" (Fleetwood *On Racial Icons* 71). Fleetwood adds that "the black celebrity icon operates in relationship to or against the limited access that blacks have had historically and presently to arenas of power, wealth and possibility," because "the black celebrity has to contend with commodity fetishization on a heightened level given the history of slavery and black bodies as commodities to be bought, sold, and exploited" (*On Racial Icons* 71). The image of a "panther in snow" is a backhanded compliment evocative of black power and black is beautiful, grounded in dehumanizing stereotypes. Slaves were supposed to be animals. The creation of animal images for Bride finds parallels in the representation of Jones as a tiger, both grounded in a long tradition of visually representing black people as exotic animals (Hobson *Venus in the Dark* 98).

In the white imaginary, black stands for comparison, as Fanon has reiterated in his seminal work *Black Skin, White Masks* (163). Bride does not occupy a site of recognition as a person. She is mere appearance. In the words of George Yancy, white is the thesis and black is its antithesis (*What White Looks Like* 9). This comparative interaction with Other, especially the black other, laid the foundation of "Hegel's famous master self that comes into being through a dialectic of recognition in a master/slave relationship" (Yancy *What White Looks* 198). According to Paget Henry, the essence of this Hegelian master self is self-consciousness, which needs to pass through the medium of another inferior self (Henry "Whiteness and Africana Phenomenology"). In fact, this self-realization comes into being after being acknowledged or recognized by the other. The image of black subalterity comes through the gaze of the master, who, like Jeri, occupies a position of authority. In this classic encounter or the dialectic of recognition, the master gaze responds "with the negating power of a racial gaze" (Henry "Whiteness and Africana Phenomenology"). The locus of this encounter or the dialectic of recognition is epidermal. It returns to the master not only recognition but confirmation of his whiteners, and for the black, the exchange returns a confirmation of his/her blackness, steeped in stereotypes, a repertoire of tropes representing his/her animality (Henry "Whiteness and Africana Phenomenology"). It is this intersubjective moment which shatters the bodily image or subjectivity of the black. This epidermal schema provides a mirror whereby the master secures/moors his whiteness and unmoors or negates the black as a dark animalistic creature. According to Fanon, "the Black [*le Noir*] no longer has to be black [noir], but must be it in the perception of the White" (qtd. in Judy 56). Meaning the White gaze can make a person black even if his/her skin is not.

Bride is not only black but an Oreo type, a person who is black on the outside but white on the inside. Although being black no longer bars access to socioeconomic opportunities, there are new modes of passing in which blacks are willing to become so-called Oreos (Kennedy *Sell-Out* 177–8). Oreo is a metaphor of passing. It is as if Jeri, having created an Oreo identity for Bride, exposes her act of passing, her interior which highlights the problem of visibility or "specularity in identity construction (internal and external—identity and corporeality—are supposed to match)" (Nerad "Introduction" 9). Racial passing disrupts the idea of fixed identities. It becomes a trope for people to admit their secret transracial sexual orientations by coming out of their closets, rather than hiding them like secret fetishes (*Dilution Anxiety* 80, 169). It highlights the cultural anxiety of assigning/fixing people into socially demarcated identities like black, gay, and other queer and closeted identities.

New Black and the Queer

Brooklyn, like a queer detective, wants to know what happened between Bride and Huxley. She wants to know if the scene of so-called child abuse that Bride witnessed involved more than the act of "seeing [Huxley] diddling the kids" (48). She wants Bride to confide whether she was molested or seduced by Huxley as a child (48). Bride seemingly rejects Brooklyn's suggestion she had an unnatural relationship with Huxley as "a secret lesbian"—as a gay or queer child afraid to acknowledge her past and hidden sexual orientation (48). Perhaps, Brooklyn wants to know this aspect of Bride's life because as a child, she was herself molested by her uncle (139). Or perhaps she simply urges Bride to be more open about her sexual orientation as her company is run practically by all sorts of identities: "bi's, straights, grannies, gays and anybody who took their look seriously" (48). In a world where sex is no longer a fetish, she urges Bride to reveal her closeted identity without any fear of exposure, persecution or scandal: "What's the point of closets these days?" (48).[1] She wants to know if Bride, as a child, had a sexual past—the kind of child who lives "liquidly, longingly, stealthily, or unconsciously in its broad array: the child queered by money, gender, sexuality, race, ghostly gayness, and imagined innocence" (Stockton "The Queer Child" 505). The deconstruction slogan "To be is to be queer" also appears in this discourse on the new black and the queer child who lives in the closet. Discussing Elizabeth Bishop's work, Frank Bidart suggests, "not to be in the closet was to be ghettoised, people might know or suspect that one was gay, but to talk about it openly in straight society was generally considered out-of-control or stupid" (qtd. in Dickie 146). The power of the new black now resides in his/her ability to come out of the closet. Closets are no longer required to preserve secret identities. Therefore, Oreo as a trope of the passing figure embraces those with closeted identities or sexualities. It reveals the pressure of the dominant culture on those people deciding whether or not to come out of the closet and admit their acts of passing or performing certain identities (Sánchez & Schlossberg *Passing* "Introduction" 6). Passing betrays one's real identity. It exposes the passer as wearing a mask or façade. It catches the person performing an identity which conflicts with his/her objective and subjective reality, because the passer is pretending to appear as something he/she is not deep inside (Nerad "Introduction" 9). The passer does not look like what he is inside or vice versa. Bride understands the implications of being the new black or how she is perceived by Brooklyn and the cultural gaze of Jeri as Oreo.

The exchange between Jeri and Bride is also evocative of du Bois' famous concept of black "double consciousness," which describes "the peculiar sensation [. . .] of always looking at one's self through the eyes of others, of measuring one's soul by a tape that looks on in amused contempt and pity" (du Bois 5). Du Bois' concept of double-consciousness, the complexities of black identity captured by the state of being Oreo, is relevant to the exchange between Jeri and Bride, in which the "white hegemony produces in African Americans an awareness of one's self that incorporates an awareness of how one is perceived by others" (Osucha "Passing in Blackface" 135). This awareness of how one is perceived by the other encompasses an awareness of one's racialized subjectivity, Bride's racialization of her subjectivity. She can read behind Jeri's efforts to exoticize her as an Oreo. These efforts reveal contemporary interests in racial classification, sketching the Fanonian historic-racial schema, which returns Bride's body or her signifying blackness in the form of a new genus, a strange new exotic creature or specimen (Yancy *Black Bodies* 71).

The significance of being compared to exotic animals is not entirely lost on Bride. Historically blacks were ranked on same level of other animals. The objective was to get them to recognize their valuation on the scale of being. Bride can read the racist categorizations and projections behind Jeri's back-handed compliments before she willingly becomes "the mimetic reflection of [Jeri's] white projections" (Yancy *Black Bodies* 159). Like Fanon, she finds herself subject to scrutiny and discovers her blackness and the incumbent stereotypes connecting her with her ancestors. Above all, she finds herself reduced to a character who sells both her blackness and her sexuality. Bride shares an affinity with "these nineties women" in *Love* who are "prostitutes" and "have always set the style" with their "success" (*Love* 4). Like "these nineties women," she prostitutes herself for "success" and discovers her immorality and that, too, in relation to whiteness or people with fairer complexions and better moral values. Tongue-in-cheek, Bride dismisses Jeri's white-on-black logic by comparing his analogies to being "Oreo." She understands how the logic behind the white-only clothes operates on the principle of debasement aesthetics rather than enhancement of her beauty. According to Stockton, "Material meant to decorate, seen as an aesthetic enrichment for the body, can visit debasement upon the wearer, even as the wearer may think she's being praised" (Stockton *Beautiful Bottom* 64). The compliment of being the new black is not entirely lost on Bride. She understands the significance of wearing white as a stigmatizing skin, which turns her inside out as an Oreo. According to Touré, an Oreo is a person who rejects blackness (Touré 33). Trey Ellis recalls how growing up in the late 80s, "it wasn't unusual to be called 'oreo' and 'nigger' on the same day" (qtd. in New 111). According to Mark Anthony Neal, to be Oreo is to be "effectively "queered" by both white and black communities for being unauthentically "black" or "white" simultaneously" (111). It is an old loaded, pejorative and stigmatized expression used for those African Americans with the physical appearance of black on the outside but who were white on the inside. Whites in America use such derogatory expressions, like coconuts used for Caribbean immigrants, to denigrate them for the alleged affront of acting white. According to J. Martin Favor, the term Oreo questions the authenticity of a person's blackness:

> The legal status of blackness, however significant, is no more culturally important than people's everyday lived experience of their own racial identity. A cursory and anecdotal glance at the subject reveals that—even outside the rules and strictures of the law—the definition of blackness is constantly being invented, policed, transgressed, and contested. When hip hop artists remind themselves and their audience to "stay black" or "keep it real," they are implicitly suggesting that there is a recognisable, repeatable, and agreed upon thing that we might call black authenticity. By the same token, one can still hear the epithet "Oreo" being tossed at certain people; generally preferred as an

insult, it suggests that such a person is black on the outside but white on the inside. The term is intended to question a person's authenticity regardless of phenotype. A dark-skinned person can be "internally white" while a light-skinned person might have all the qualities of "real blackness." Furthermore, the "Oreo" insult implies that the definition of blackness itself has foundations outside physical pigmentation.

(qtd. in Wilkinson 107)

To borrow a Fanonian expression, these people want to whiten their race because they suffer from what he calls the epidermalization or lactification complex. This is also the logic behind Derrida's concept of white mythology, i.e., to enact a life of whiteness, to turn white or live a life according to the logic of white desire. Being Oreo no longer refers to what the novelist Colson Whitehead explains as, "What was called oreoness ten to twenty years ago is being who you are and being comfortable with doing what you want and not caring about what other people think. Being called an oreo was stupid then and it's stupid now. People are more aware that those categories are dumb. If you are an authentic person, true to who you are and how you're wired, then like what you like" (qtd. in Touré 55–6). Bride cannot escape the lure of Oreoness or "the colour fetish," and is conscious of her appearance or mask as she tries to adjust her lifestyle according to the shades of Fanon's "white whiteness." The definitions or shades of whiteness reveal Bride's obsession with whiteness in terms of social aspiration. Lilia Moritz Schwarcz describes the Brazilian obsession with whiteness:

Definitions such as very white, white, reddish-white, white molasses, white brunette, blond, pushing white (puxa-para-branca), pale white, light blond, freckled white, Blondie, dirty white, whitened, regular, and a little whitened show how, out of the flexibility of concepts, one great projection is symbolically expressed. When one is not white, one may attempt to be.

(Schwarcz 83)

This is not a critique of blind consumerism but of how to maintain one's personality within the norms of a socially acceptable lifestyle. Bride becomes a victim of internalized colorism. She shapes her existence and becomes a prisoner of color. Living according to shades of whiteness subjects her life to a metamorphosis: "True or not. It made me, remade me" (36). Passing for white does not merge her "into a better, truer self" (Hobbs 132). It offers her a life of economic success and social privilege, even a transformational opportunity at self-fashioning, but at a terrible price. Living according to the white imaginary reduces her to an object of desire, to a mode of being unseen except as an object. Her human interaction and racial relationships are based on economic relations alone. Nobody sees her subjectivity beyond her physicality and the principle of economy. Except for "waiting for my crotch or paycheck," "none [was] interested in what I thought, just what I looked like (36–7)".

New Black and Oreotization

Morrison critiques the objectification of women. Even though the issues of black upward mobility appear to be racially more egalitarian in the novel, they still require women come to terms with their commodified body image as they struggle to have their subjectivity appreciated and validated. For example, Bride does not question Jeri's motives. She relinquishes her choices and subjectivity and embraces white standards of beauty through her body to gain acceptance in the white world of business. According to Paul C. Taylor, such blind embrace of white beauty standards, what he calls "white-oriented somatic aesthetics" or somaesthetics of black bodies is "perfectly compatible with denial of personhood and rights, especially when male supremacy and racist stereotypes linger" (Taylor P. *Black is Beautiful* 167). Most, like Jeri, disregard Bride as a person. They sexualize, objectify and exploit her without any consideration for her feelings or desires. She curtails her choice, her lifestyle and even her eating habits according to Jeri's advice. She mentally transitions into whiteness so fluidly she does not realize her conditioning. Whiteness disciplines and shapes her body and self-image. She internalizes whiteness to such a self-denigrating degree that she becomes white in her appearance, mind and even daily habits. She wants to benefit from appearing white even at the cost of her compromising subjectivity and personhood. According to Fanon, when the black subject tries to adapt his/her lifestyle to the technique and style of the white man, instead of being natural, it erodes and negates the personality in "an avalanche of murders" (Yancy *What White Looks* 204).

Fanon critiques, just like Morrison, the willingness of the racialized subject to compromise and cover their black bodies in "white masks." As Paget Henry observes, "These masks increase the need for precisely the kind of white recognition that is not forthcoming from the master self. This need is not for the confirmation of one's blackness, but for the confirmation of one's humanity as a self-conscious and autonomous existence" (Henry "Whiteness and Africana Phenomenology"). Society does not return this kind of confirmation to Bride. Like Pecola from *The Bluest Eye*, she becomes a victim of the pervasive ideological representation of value-laden whiteness or what George Yancy defines in his study of *The Bluest Eyes* as the white aesthetic ideals (*What White Looks Like* 19, 129). It is one thing to change one's appearance according to the beauty standards for black women, like straight hair as a marker of elite status, along with light skin, in order to "maximise their potential for beauty," and enter elite social spaces and achieve greater upward mobility; it is entirely another thing to change one's appearance according to the historically informed, white sedimentary images of anti-black iconography and visibility. Like Pecola, she has internalized the fiction that whiteness is the norm of societal acceptance and beauty and the key to material success. She becomes a prisoner of whiteness like Pecola as she molds her life according to the discursive power of whiteness and its violence. Like Pecola, who buys Mary Jane candy and drinks milk out of a Shirley Temple mug, Bride, too, tries to ingest whiteness by eating and wearing white. Shirley Temple represents the aesthetic of white idealized blue-eyed beauty for Pecola. Equally important is Pecola's ritual of drinking white milk from the mug. According to Yancy, "Milk is symbolic of whiteness" (*What White Looks Like* ch. 5). It is not that Pecola "consumes so much milk, rather, it is out of her need to *become* white through the very act of consuming the milk" (*What White Looks Like* ch. 5). It is the power in the whiteness of the milk that Pecola seeks. Perhaps the whiteness in the milk will create a metamorphosis, a transubstantiation, and change her from black to white, from absent to present, from nothing to something. This theme of ingesting whiteness is obvious when Pecola goes to buy some Mary Jane candies. Even this innocent act becomes an opportunity for self-resentment and self-denigration. Yancy quotes Morrison on Pecola's desire for whiteness to support his argument:

> Each pale yellow wrapper has a picture on it. A picture of little Mary Jane, for whom the candy is named. Smiling white face. Blond hair in gentle disarray, *blue eyes* looking at her out of a world of *clean comfort*. The eyes are petulant, mischievous. To Pecola they are simply *pretty*. To eat the candy is somehow *to eat the eyes, eat Mary Jane. Love Mary Jane. Be Mary Jane.*
>
> (qtd. in *What White Looks Like* ch. 5)

Yancy adds, "Like the whiteness of the milk, the piece of candy is believed to have the power to effect a genuine state of ontological alterity, changing Pecola from black to white" (*What White Looks Like* ch. 5). The tyranny of whiteness is that "blacks internalize a set of values or practices that create a form of self-resentment" (Yancy *What White Looks Like* ch. 5).

The beauty industry in the West especially has commercialized a white concept of beauty by investing heavily in white images of beauty. Advertisements for creams and beauty soaps exploit and parody blackness for racial advantage or white supremacy. Alice Hall quotes the example of an advertisement for Sunlight Soap with "a caricatured image of a very black child to make a point about the power of a detergent to achieve an idealized, pure 'whiteness'" (Hall 71). Morrison denounces the aesthetic ideal of white beauty. She considers the romantic concept of physical beauty as "one of the dumbest, most pernicious and destructive ideas of the Western world" (qtd. in Stern). She illustrates the destructive impact of white standards of beauty, from *The Bluest Eye* to *God Help the Child*. Bride internalizes Jeri's advice to wear all white so that it becomes a reactive force in her own existence through a process of white discipline and indoctrination. She becomes a queer of color who cannot resist the lure of whiteness. Like Pecola, she fully internalizes the seductive aesthetics of white beauty in her daily life as a form of universal normality. Instead of freeing herself from the tyranny of whiteness or what Morrison describes as the "self-destruction of colorism," she surrenders herself to the panoptic gaze of whiteness and tries to discipline her lifestyle according to Jeri's perception rather than refusing to become a prisoner of whiteness. To borrow an expression from Foucault's analysis of sexuality, she gives in to "the deep internalization of a carefully orchestrated value-laden understanding of the self" (qtd. in Yancy *What White Looks Like* ch. 5). By disciplining herself through the strict regime of the white code, she creates a very destructive self-identity. She is so enthralled by the logic of whiteness that it results in the total erosion of her subjectivity. She becomes so Oreo-ish that she not only wears white or acts, thinks or feels white; she even orders and eats white, perhaps in order to become more white. On her way to find Booker, she orders food in a restaurant like this:

> "May I have a white omelette, no cheese?"
> "White? You mean no eggs?"
> "No. No yolks."

(81)

On another occasion, she is fascinated by the shades of whiteness:

> At first it was boring shopping for white-only clothes until I learned how many shades of white there were: ivory, oyster, alabaster, paper white, snow, cream, ecru, Champagne, ghost, bone. Shopping got even more interesting when I began choosing colors for accessories.

(33)

Like Pecola, her desire to appreciate whiteness, eat and wear white only, betrays a desire to possess and value the aesthetic beauty of whiteness (Yancy *What White Looks Like* ch. 5). In South Asian countries like India and parts of Sri Lanka, where the color white is invested with value, it is customary for pregnant women to drink white coconut water as it is believed it can whiten the skin of the baby's skin before it is born. Bride's habit of eating white reflects a similar epidermal complex, compelling her to eat and wear white out of the desire to become white. Jeri's comparisons of Bride to exotic animals suggest a sublimation of the black. Like a connoisseur of taste, he uses a rich vocabulary of confectionery to underscore Bride's black (edible) essence. His metaphors of white and black produce a Fanonian "epidermal-racial schema": "I see in those white faces that it is not a new man who has come in, but a new kind of man, a new genus" (Fanon 87). It is not because her name is Bride that she should always wear white, but because of the charm it adds to her "licorice skin," and as the new black she is "more Hershey's syrup than licorice. Makes people think of whipped cream and chocolate soufflé every time they see (her)" (33). Each time they see her it reminds them of something exotic and edible. No wonder wherever she goes she is admired by "stunned but *hungry eyes*" (emphasis added, 34). Just like when bell hooks enters a dessert place and encounters a group of white people who "all burst into laughter and point to a row of gigantic chocolate breasts complete with nipples—huge edible tits" (*Black Looks* 61). According to hooks, the new black image caters to a cultural imaginary eager to reinscribe the image of black women as sexual commodities (73). She adds: "This new representation is a response to contemporary fascination with an ethnic look, with the exotic Other who promises to fulfill racial and sexual stereotypes, to satisfy longings. This image is but an extension of the edible black tit" (*Black Looks* 73).

Drawing heavily on animal imagery, Jeri eroticizes and exoticizes Bride's black body, making her "a kind of human-animal hybrid" (Peterson *Bestial Traces* 17): "All sable and white. A panther in snow. And with your body? And those wolverine eyes? Please!" (34). What can Bride not achieve through the sheer force of her exotic body and its charms? Jeri invests her body with exoticism and successfully helps Bride to commodify it because: "Black sells. It's the hottest commodity in the civilised world. White girls, even brown girls strip naked to get that kind of attention" (36). The new black has become the flip side of desirability. Jeri sells darker-skinned blackness as desirable compared to whiteness, which used to be the norm. This is a shocking statement, evocative of "old stereotypes which make the assertion of black female sexuality and prostitution synonymous" (hooks *Black Looks* 69). Jeri constructs Bride's identity, in fact, her blackness, as a comparison. As bell hooks reminds us, a black female body gains attention only when it is eroticized and projected as sexually licentious in comparison to other women (hooks *Black Looks* 66). According to Trimiko Melancon, "black women have been cast as embodying the polarized opposite of an idealized white womanhood in order to sustain such a construction as a model, if even illusory and contrived, of 'normative' womanhood" (Melancon 18). She adds that black women as the comparative "other" stand "outside the parameters of acceptability" as they are associated with excessive illicit sexuality, considered to be outside the behavioral, moral and sexual convention (Melancon 18).

According to Trimiko Melancon, popular American discourse has categorized the white women as "emblems of purity and lacking in sexuality (putative justification for the constructions of black women's and men's sexuality, as well as their respective sexual dehumanization" (Melancon 30). Jeri's comments link Bride to illicit and licentious sexuality. By "Black sells," he implies sex sells. The black as an object of sex, as a stripper, as a concubine, as a project chick, sells. Black bodies and their sexualities are commodities. Bride's blackness functions as a commodity depending upon what adorns her body rather than what is within it. First and foremost, Bride embodies a blackness which is a sellable commodity in the eyes of Jeri. He negatively colorizes her blackness in comparison with other women. Next, he envisages her as a stripper against whom white women and women of color have to outstrip or devalue or debase themselves. Jeri's misogynistic logic debases and devalues white women and women of color equally. He fits all women into a competition through which women are devalued or presented negatively and stereotypically. Jeri, the image-maker, not only creates and promotes the stereotypical images projected onto the black body and enhances its exaggerated exoticism, but also perpetuates the notion that black chicks are not only chic, but debased and loose. White girls and women of color would have to be nude themselves and sell their bodies like pros faced with the challenge of Bride's body, to vie for attention— stripping naked to compete is the ultimate degradation of the female entity. Jeri circumscribes Bride's autonomy and obliterates her subjectivity by turning her into a commodity with the highest market value.

Jeri's formulation of the new black and his attempt to commodify Bride's body concurs with bell hooks' observation that the commodification of the black body by the dominant American culture is as "the strong bitchified black woman who is on the make" (hooks *Black Looks* 69).[2] There was a time when black women had to develop a stronger style and project a stronger image to vie for attention and recognition. Now the exotic look of the new black is especially profitable for companies. To outperform in the corporate world of business and the job market, they have to carry a likeable personality. Bride does not resist Jeri's loaded images of sexual stereotypes in order to empower herself socially as the new black but embraces the oreotization of her body for greater economic success and social respectability. Convinced by the cultural imperative to wear white only, Bride wears nothing "to detract from what Jeri calls [her] black-coffee-and-whipped-cream palette. A panther in snow" (50). Bride's willingness to accept the dictates of Jeri has its roots in her childhood, the subject of next chapter.

Notes

1. In *Dilution Anxiety and the Black Phallus*, Margo Natalie Crawford discusses James Baldwin and homosexuality in his fiction like *Tell Me*. According to Crawford, "Baldwin insists that there is no rift between 'Black is Beautiful' and 'black is gay.'" She also mentions Eve Sedgwick who recalls National Public Radio discussions of 1960s as "the decade when Black people came out of the closet." Returning to Baldwin, Crawford mentions that for Baldwin "coming out of the closet" is more than a trope for the Black Power movement when he explores, in *Tell Me*, the inseparability of the "racial closet" and the "sexual closet." Is Brooklyn stretching the trope of closet in her insinuation that Bride should come out of her closet? Morrison leaves it for readers to ponder if this includes the possibility of Stockton's gay and queer child "based on the model of the ghostly gay child, among other versions of children's queerness" ("The Queer Child" 507). Stockton also calls this "ghostly gay child" a "creature of delay" who could come out of the closet or "state itself publicly" after something or someone else "came out" ("The Queer Child" 507). In *The Queer Child: Or Growing Sideways in the Twentieth Century*, Stockton defines the queer child as the protogay child who emerges "through an act of retrospection and after a death [. . .]. That is to say, in one's teens or twenties, whenever (parental) plans for the child's straight designation have died, 'homosexual child,' or even 'gay child,' may finally, retrospectively, be applied. 'I am not straight.': 'I was a gay child'" (6–7).
2. Consider Helena Andrews' memoir *Bitch is the New Black*.

4   The New Black Melancholy

"These children have been tampered with."
(Toni Morrison's great grandmother in *The Origin of Others*)

Child Abuse and the Myth of the Eroticized Child

Bride was six years of age when she witnessed the traumatizing act of Mr. Leigh, the white landlord, subjecting a neighborhood boy child to sexual abuse. She shared this with her mother, who was more interested in keeping their apartment than standing up for the boy, because standing up to Leigh meant finding another place to live:

> She wasn't interested in tiny fists or big hairy thighs; she was interested in keeping our apartment. She said, "Don't you say a word about it. Not to anybody, do you hear me Lula? Forget it. Not a single word."
>
> (54–5)

Bride became so afraid she forgot to tell her mother the entire account, including what she heard Mr. Leigh shout upon noticing that Bride was watching him abuse the child: "Hey, little black cunt! Close that window and get the fuck outta here!" (55). At the formative age of six, Bride would have retained this as the most traumatic event in her life and will enact a series of traumatic reenactments in response to this moment of original trauma. Later on, she will receive a barrage of racially loaded vocabulary "with mysterious definitions but clear meanings," such as "Coon. Topsy. Clinkertop. Sambo. Ooga booga" (56). She will even let her school fellows treat her "like a freak, strange, soiling like a spill of ink on white paper" (56). Afraid of complaining to the teacher "for the same reason Sweetness cautioned me about Mr. Leigh—I might get suspended or even expelled," she lets "the name-calling, the bullying travel like poison [. . .] with no antibiotic available" (56-7).

Trauma is not fully comprehensible, available or assimilable at the moment of its occurrence. Even though it is not readily accessible to consciousness, trauma stays latent and returns after "delayed appearance" with all its disruptive power and "points to the original event or at least our response to the original event" (Barnaby 39). According to Cathy Caruth, "the story of trauma" is "the narrative of belated experience" (*Unclaimed Experience* 7). In the light of trauma theory, Bride's story is a reenactment of bearing witness against Sofia Huxley—a reenactment of the original scene of trauma, having suppressed the memories of the original trauma from the moment it occurred. The temporal gap between the original event and its latency is defined by Caruth as a "collapse of witnessing" (qtd. in Gana 161). Bride herself explains the reason behind her testifying against Sofia as response to the original event when she witnessed Mr. Leigh sexually abusing the boy. As Caruth points out, the experience of trauma "stubbornly persists in bearing witness to some forgotten wound" (*Unclaimed Experience* 5). Bride was not mature enough to take account of the event. The original scene of trauma escaped her understanding. It was not known to her in the first instance. When she wanted "truth" and "clarity," she confused Sofia Huxley with Mr. Leigh. Unwittingly, she reenacted the event she could not leave unless it was resolved: "What if it was the landlord my finger was really pointing at in that courtroom? What that teacher was accused of like what Mr. Leigh did. Was I pointing at the idea of him?" (56). The allegations against the teacher are actually the allegations against Mr. Leigh and his heinous crime of child abuse. The school teacher was only a victim of or replacement for what Mr. Leigh did. Instead of pointing her finger at the real perpetrator of child abuse, Bride points out the teacher at the behest of her mother and society, to please them. Morrison critiques the behavior of society and the failure of the system to bring to justice the real sexual predators and pedophiles, who make children the victims of their abuse. She especially highlights the most common form of child abuse that originates in the family, as in *The Bluest Eye* and *Love*, and those people whose behavior goes unsuspected merely because they enjoy the repute of being well-known and trusted in that community, as she demonstrates with the pedophile Humboldt (whose name evokes professor Humbert from Vladimir Nabokov's novel *Lolita*) and who, in *God Help the Child*, is perceived as "the nicest man in the world" (118–9). Beneath the veneer there is a dark and sinister underside. More than 90% of cases of child abuse involve someone, like a relative or community member, who is well known. She exposes the abusive and sexually predatory behavior of those who enjoy being seen as respectable and trustworthy people. She also exposes the creepy/queer behavior and sexual voyeurism of adult sex abusers of children, who take sexual gratification by looking at them. She emphasizes the consequences of sexual abuse on the impressionable minds of the very young, how sexual abuse permeates their mental landscapes and leaves permanent marks (DeSalvo 6): "What you do to children matters. And they might never forget" (43).

Morrison's description of sexually abused children shares affinities with Virginia Woolf's description of child abuse and its harmful impact upon children in the novel *To the Lighthouse*, in which Mrs. Ramsay thinks, like the narrator in *God Help the Child*, that "children never forget" their childhood, certainly not the abuse that takes place in their lives (DeSalvo 1). It is not merely a truism that what happens to children in their childhood shapes the entire trajectory of their later lives. Childhood is the key to understanding the psychic makeup of the adult. In her previous novels, like *Love*, Morrison debunked the myth of the erotic child. James Kincaid, in his book *Erotic Innocence: The Culture of Child Molesting*, makes the bold statement that "our culture has enthusiastically sexualised the child" at the expense of denying that there are adults who are sexually drawn toward vulnerable children and abuse them remorselessly (Kincaid 13). Morrison, like Kincaid, exposes the invasive and predatory voyeurism of those monsters who prey on and enjoy power over vulnerable children, a power sanctioned or concealed in societies because the pedophiles enjoy the persona of trustworthy people, like ministers of religion in the UK, US and rest of the world. Surprisingly enough, Joe Trace in *Jazz* is described in similar terms because of his trustworthiness: "A nice, neighbourly, everybody-knows-him man. The kind you let in your house because he was not dangerous because you had seen him with children [. . .] and never heard a scrap of gossip about him do wrong" (73). According to child abuse specialist, Alice Miller, the child in his or her vulnerability inadvertently awakens feelings of power and sexual aggression in pedophiles and becomes their studied and targeted sexual object. Pedophiles use the weaknesses of children to attract and exploit them sexually, as does Mr. Humboldt in *God Help the Child*, who uses his terrier to attract the children. In their warped minds, pedophiles think children need what they want to give them. Kathryn Stockton has coined the term "reverse paedophilia" to describe how society cultivates and grooms this sexual(ized) child "for our own purposes" ("The Queer Child" 506). According to Stockton, reverse paedophilia places desire on the object turning "innocence upside down": "Somewhere a child is desiring me, so I imagine, so I'm led to feel" ("The Queer Child" 506). Morrison creates scenes of "reverse paedophilia" most noticeably in *Love* and *God Help the Child*. In these novels, the paedophilic desire is "aimed not by an adult at child [. . .] but by a child at an adult" (Stockton "The Queer Child" 506). Paedophilic desires in children are projected as latent and waiting to be aroused by adults.

Morrison emphasizes the need for practical and educational steps to educate and warn children they can be abused without being aware of it, for example, through voyeurism, as perverted pedophiles are drawn toward them sexually. The best example of such child sexual abuse and sexploitation comes from Morrison's earliest novels like *The Bluest Eye*, her middle novel, *Jazz*, and later novel, *Love*. In *Love*, Morrison exposes how adults, like Bill Cosey, are sexually attracted to children. Cosey gets interested in a teenage girl, Heed, a childhood friend of his granddaughter, Christine. He marries her when she is barely eleven. His marriage becomes the cause of resentment amongst his family members and a source of gossip for the town. It finally becomes the reason for the disintegration of his business when Cosey dies at age eighty-one (*Love* 37). Cosey spots Heed in the hotel, presumably, wiggling her hips "and in awe" to the sound of music as she moves down the hallway to fetch the jacks she wants to play with Christine at the beach (*Love* 190): "She bumps into her friend's grandfather," who "touches her chin, and then casually, [. . .] her nipple, or rather the place under her swimsuit where a nipple will be if the circle dot on her chest ever changes" (*Love* 191). Heed is obviously fondled and abused sexually before she can even realize this has happened to her. She finds herself unable to comprehend the experience and is even unable to share it with her friend, Christine: "Heed can't speak, can't tell her friend what happened" (*Love* 191). Child abuse disrupts the normal developmental trajectory of a child and it is experienced "as a loss for the child at the time and for the rest of her life" (O'Dell 136). What is interesting to observe is the representation of an erotically charged, pleasure-seeking, and sexually inciting child who encourages and incites adults to arouse and groom them sexually. Here Morrison highlights the inverse picture of child abuse: that all forms of sexual abuse are expressions of power, the adult's power to coerce and incite. Child sexual abuse is a powerful issue, and the question of adult responsibility or the motivation of the pedophile has to be understood within the strategies of power that motivate him. Consider the portrait of Heed as a wicked girl who is waiting to be aroused:

> So there is something wrong with Heed. The old man saw it right away so all he had to do was touch her and it moved as he knew it would because the wrong was already there, waiting for a thumb to bring it to life. And she had started it—not him. The hip-wiggling came first—then him.
>
> (*Love* 192)

Again, the projection here is of an erotic and sexually charged child, who in her polymorphous sexuality, waits to be fondled and sexually aroused, while the adult is not held accountable for his perverse desire to arouse sexuality in children. Mar Gallego convincingly discussed Cosey's sexual arousal, his intentional fondling of Heed and his "pedophilic intentions" reflected in his desire to groom the teenage girl Heed, "to his taste" and how he introduces his own granddaughter Christine "to nasty and blames it on her" (Gallego 95–9). However, the most interesting aspect of the novel verges on the paedophilic attractions he feels for almost all the women in his life, including Junior, over whom his ghostly presence presides as an insatiable pedophile voyeur, deriving paedophilic gratification by watching Junior copulate with her boyfriend, Romen. The characterization of Cosey as an insatiable sexual voyeur in his afterlife corresponds with how he behaved when alive. For example, his interest in Heed's "hip-wiggling," which tempts him. Even in their final verdict on the character and legacy of Cosey, the public do not accuse him of perversion, but vilify Heed, as if she were the original temptress, and vindicate Cosey: "They forgave Cosey. Everything. Even to the point of blaming a child for a grown man's interest in her" (*Love* 147). However, the narrator continuously reminds the reader Cosey was "The dirty one who introduced (Heed) to nasty and blamed it on her" (165). Bill Cosey, like Joe Trace and Mr. Humboldt, come from the gallery of so-called unsuspicious and trustworthy old reprobates, dirty old men and pedophiles who subject their child victims to their constant scopophiliac gaze (*Love* 116–8–9) and "can't imagine anything more majestic to a child than their own (projected) selves" (*Love* 199) and finally lead them to taste of the Biblical apple.[1] The perverted adults who see children as objects of their paedophilia fail to see anything other than projections of their own fantasies and perversions.

Bride, like Heed's friend, Christine—who witnesses the revolting primal scene in which her grandfather Cosey fondled Heed first and masturbates afterwards—witnesses the abject moment of child sexual abuse. She shares her traumatic experience of witnessing child abuse with Booker to make sense of and find some solace as she struggles to overcome her ethical dilemma of having wrongfully convicted Sofia Huxley. According to Judith Herman, "sharing the traumatic experience is a precondition for the restitution of a sense of meaningful World" (qtd. in Stow 223). Sharing her traumatic confidences with Booker, Bride reorients her life. Booker advises her to come out of her cocoon and share her experience with as many people as possible. This is his way of suggesting how to come to terms with her past traumas of witnessing child abuse by placing it in the public realm. This helped Bride develop a new understanding of self-resilience and spreading of awareness.[2] Sharing the intimate moments of her life with Booker, Bride found catharsis, an outlet for her pent-up emotions and relief: "More than that. [She] felt curried, safe, owned" (56). Above all, she discovered herself as an embodied woman. Booker's love adds to her confidence, her joy, her subjectivity and capacity to enjoy and explore her sexuality. After the sudden breakup, she asked: "Why would he leave her stripped of all comfort, emotional security?" (79). Full of confidence as she is in her accomplishments and exotic beauty, she still feels jilted and spurned. She undergoes a metamorphosis, a regression to a prepubescent state, to being the atavistic "[scared] little black girl" or "too-black little girl" (97, 140, 142, 144), the source of shame for her parents. Jean Wyatt reads in this regression to a childlike state "a corporeal representation of her temptation to remain the child victim of trauma" (184)—"to remain the little black girl cruelly unloved by a colorist mother" (182).

Morrison dramatizes this state of regression through the gradual loss of pubic hair, and downsizing of her body, including the breasts she prized as the source of her empowerment and femininity. The loss of hair becomes a metaphor for a literal loss or erasure of her agency/subjectivity and sanity. Most of her bodily transformation takes place at the level of hallucinations. Jean Wyatt links Bride's bodily transformation, in the wake of Booker's rejection of Bride, as reenactment of the initial scenes of trauma in which her mother refused to touch or nurture her daughter. However, her hallucinations trigger bodily loss of self-image, especially after Booker's desertion of Bride. Therefore, her hallucinations can also be described as a form of hallucinatory melancholia in response to her loss of love or Booker's harsh criticism of Bride as not being the woman he wants. She finds Booker to be the source of her illness and suffering: "[. . .] when she touched the place where her breasts used to be the humming changed to sobs. That's when she understood that the body changes began not simply after he left, but because he left" (93–4). She thinks she is literally losing her pubic hair, which is the opposite of puberty and womanhood. It is as if she is reverting, like Benjamin Button in *The Curious Case of Benjamin Button* by F. Scott Fitzgerald, to a state of childhood. She sets out, cultivating her self-respect, "to stand up for herself and confront the first person she had bared her soul to" in order to "force him to explain why she didn't deserve better treatment from him, and, second, what did he mean by "you are not the woman" (80). In an attempt to take control of her agency and personal dignity, she departs from the script of the conventional compromising woman who was historically denied agency, like her mother, who is disparagingly viewed as a welfare queen, and finds herself incapable of asserting her dignity and self-respect (Thompson L. 24). She discovers Booker's whereabouts from an envelope addressed to him by Salvatore Ponti, to whom he owes money. According to Ponti, Booker lives in a place called Whiskey. Speeding and disoriented en route to Whiskey, Bride loses control of her Jaguar and has a terrible accident. She finds herself at the mercy of a family living an idyllic life divested of material possessions. The family has three members: Steve, Evelyn and their adopted daughter, Rain, whom they found in the rain.

Rain is another example in this novel replete with stories of abused children. She shares her own story of being prostituted and thrown out by her birth mother. This prompts Bride to question mothering, maternal neglect and the need for nurture: "Why? Why would she do that?" (101). Rain, who had no sympathetic and supportive person to talk to, shares her own story of child abuse with Bride: how her mother sold her to one of her "regular" customers for paid sex. The bare details of child abuse revolt Bride and make her repeat: "How could anybody do that to a child, any child, and one's own?" (102). This stringent criticism makes Bride ask Rain what she would say if she saw her mother again. Rain said nothing; she would rather decapitate her mother, and seems to take sadistic delight in imagining it. Symbolically, she punishes her mother for her cruelty. This exchange between Bride and Rain perhaps sums up best the initial title of the novel as *The Wrath of Children* (Chen). Morrison's original title emphasized the need to recognize the wrath of children in the form of reactive hatred and violent aggression as realistic reactions to life-changing and traumatic experiences of child sexual abuse. Morrison presents the reader with a realistic portrayal of the intensity of rage felt by a child traumatized by sexual abuse compared to adults, who can experience such emotions with more restraint. Children need sympathetic or supportive company, like Bride, in order to express their pent-up emotions lest their neglect and bottled up rage become all the more violent if they are unable to express them. Once the reader is able to empathize with Rain, as Bride does, they are able to understand the reactive nature of her sadistic fantasies of violence and dismemberment.

Morrison concurs with child abuse specialists like Alice Miller, that a child's wrath is appropriate to her situation, as it is free from transference, i.e., directed at the person who has inflicted pain and abuse unlike adults' reactive hatred, which can be directed at a substitute object. An example of displaced discharge of unrestrained adult aggression is Valerian Sweet, who tortures her only child, her son, in response to the hatred she stores up in her heart against her husband in *Tar Baby*. Another example is Claudia, from *The Bluest Eye*, who directs her reactive aggression onto a Shirley Temple doll, which she dismembers in order to understand the secret of her appeal and magic. Bride empathizes with Rain and gives her an outlet for her emotions. By listening to her with sympathetic attention, Bride understands that Rain's grief will die of its own accord and change itself into a healthy constructive self-defense when she no longer experiences her rage as meaningless, but as an appropriate response to sexual abuse. Bride experienced such moments of release as an adult when she shared her grief with Booker. As Miller observes, a child who has been abused has to break the taboo to become aware and talk about it lest she feels robbed of her self-confidence (Miller A. 67). Rain and her reactive behavior have to be understood in the sociocultural context of her child abuse, the power dynamics within the family and society at large, the lack of conscience of the parent(s), who subject their children to sexual abuse, mistreatment, humiliation and the narcissistic wounds the latter inflicts on the child (Miller A. 60). The reader can then reach a deeper understanding of the reactive nature of the child's aggressive behavior rather than attribute it to the existence of, say, the Freudian death instinct or the perverse nature of children's sexuality. It is no wonder Rain comes to develop a bond with Bride, who has the ability to understand the nature of Rain's reality. No wonder Rains finds Bride's company psychologically generative, considers her to be her sister and misses her company long after she is gone. Unlike Jeri, she lionizes Bride as *her black lady*. By risking her life to defend Rain, Bride demonstrates that she embodies the dignity and self-respect which are the true hallmarks of the black lady (Thompson L. 24).

The Paradox of Memorialization

The next part of my discussion revolves around Booker, his past life, his aspirations as a student, his family life and the loss of his favorite brother, Adam, also a victim of child abuse. The narrative focuses on Booker's inconsolable state of mourning, which affected his family and interpersonal relationships and how he finally overcame his mourning. As Simon Stow observes, ever since the publication of Freud's essay "Mourning and Melancholia," Western understanding of mourning and response to grief and loss have been influenced by his magisterial work (Stow 4) and its subsequent modifications by theorists like Nicolas Abraham and Jacques Derrida, who are all highly indebted to Freud's original work. My discussion of Booker's melancholy in response to the loss of his brother relates to the Freudian tenets of melancholy and their development into political or democratic (social or communal) mourning, which I refer as the new black melancholy.

Adam's decaying body is discovered "in a culvert" (114). The "very excess" of his brother's ostentatious funeral makes Booker feel "lonelier." He felt his brother was being "buried again, suffocating under song, sermon, tears, crowds and flowers" (114). To him, his brother's death was not an occasion for rituals of ceremony and grief. It called for a democratic response for mourning and the demand for justice. McIvor defines democratic mourning as a civic obligation or open democratic dynamic, embodying an ongoing labor of recognition and repair in face of the experience of social loss, trauma, violence, disrespect, devaluation of life, marginalization and other instances of social injustice (McIvor 89).[3] People need the democratic practices of mourning, monuments or public memorialization through which the trauma of social loss and racial wounds can be redressed and worked through (McIvor 113), particularly in the second decade of twenty-first century defined by the need to build or erect reparative/ reconciliatory memorials or demolish Confederate statues or memorials.[4]

Booker's effort to engage/mobilize people and to memorialize his brother indicates his desire to protest and expose the shortcomings of American democracy and legal systems, like the judiciary and the police. Like a revolutionary, he wants to challenge and reinvigorate law enforcement institutions to take stock of themselves through the rituals of the political act of public mourning. Drawing upon African American political responses to disposable human loss in face of social injustice, his act of political mourning and attempt to memorialize represents the quest for equitable civil rights by resistance against the unjust denial and postponement of justice. According to Stow, such instances of political responses to loss and grief were "central to fight against slavery and post-Reconstruction violence, and to the [ongoing] struggle for civil rights" (Stow 57). In the absence of democratic or public mourning, which adds to the feelings/intensity of loss, Booker withdraws into an introverted state of blocked grief, into the state of post-melancholy or new black melancholy, making it difficult for him to overcome his grief, mourning and sadness. In fact, he suffers from a paradox of mourning which is both private and public, individual and social, with greater emphasis on the isolated nature of subjective mourning: "He wanted to redirect the mourning—make it private, social and, most of all, his alone" (115). Booker's mother's (and his family's) refusal to publicly mourn and the former's desire to monumentalize the death of Adam can be read in connection with two of the most pivotal acts of public and private loss and social grievance in African American history.[5]

Firstly, the context of grief resonates with Mamie Till Mobley, mother of Emmett Till who was murdered in 1955. Mobley did not want to "keep private grief private" (McIvor "Preface"). After Emmett Till's mutilated body was recovered from the Thallahatchie River, "[she] requested an open coffin and allowed photographs to be taken and published of her dead son's disfigured body" (Rankine 148). Like Booker, she wanted to bring it into the public realm "as a new kind of logic" (Rankine 148). According to Rankine, "Mobley's refusal to keep private grief private allowed a body that meant nothing to the criminal-justice system to stand as evidence [. . .] by insisting we look with her upon the dead, she reframed mourning as a method of acknowledgement that helped energize the civil rights movement in the 1950s and '60s" (Rankine 148). Booker, like Mobley, wants to make mourning part of day-to-day life to acknowledge the struggle for equality and justice—a desire that Booker wants to rekindle in the post-civil rights

context of mass incarceration, rampant child abuse, sexual violence, enduring poverty, social neglect, deep interracial (mis)trust and the partial legal/
judiciary system. The social reaction to Emmett's loss led to the civil rights
movement.

Secondly, we can connect Adam's loss to Michael Brown's and Trayvon
Martin's deaths (and perhaps the unresolved deaths of other black youths).
Brown's mother, Lesley McSpadden, unlike Mobley, did not want her son's
mutilated body exposed to the media or to be made a public spectacle.
Instead, she, like Booker's mother, wanted her son to be covered and buried
rather than to be campaigned for, commodified into "modes of capitalism"
(Rankine 153).[6] Brown's and Martin's death resulted in the Black Lives
Matter movement, whose protests represent not simply an effort to mourn
the particular deaths of Freddie Gray, Trayvon Martin or Michael Brown
but are an "attempt to keep mourning an open dynamic in our culture"
(McIvor "Afterword").

To borrow from the psychoanalytical writings of Nicolas Abraham and
Maria Torok on Mourning and Melancholia, Booker mourns and introjects his dead brother to such an extent that his "mourning erects a secret
tomb" inside his being (Abraham & Torok 130). According to Abraham
and Torok, the act of entombment objectifies the "fantasy of incorporation"
(Abraham & Torok 132). Identification with the "objectal loss" is so strong
that the dead and the aggrieved become one (Abraham & Torok 111). It is
as if the aggrieved becomes possessed by the subject of his/her loss. In their
grief over the lost love-object, "they lend their own flesh to their phantom
object of love" (Abraham & Torok 136). Booker had not considered himself independently from his brother since they were born. It seems as if he
were in a symbiotic "dual-relation," not based upon what Hungarian ana-
lyst Imre Hermann described as "mother-child unity" (qtd. in Secret 141),
but a unity with his brother, which is so pure and innocent that it requires
the love of an angel to guard and protect it. This is why Booker calls for
public mourning and monumentalization, so that the loss of innocence and
purity can be acknowledged and worked through. Lack of familial mourning or a monument in memory of Adam increases his sense of social injustice and familial distrust. After Adam is gone, he is unable to recover from
the loss of his brother. In a Freudian sense, he is unable to assimilate the
loss of his brother into his psyche and finds it difficult to invest in himself
(James R. 18, 162). Booker refuses to accept a substitute for his brother,
and holds unto his image. His act of mourning becomes narcissistic and
egotistical. In remembrance of his brother Adam, whom he considers "a
flawless replacement," and a reincarnation of his twin brother "who didn't
take a single living breath," Booker "had a small rose tattooed on his left
shoulder" (120). Having a tattoo is one of his attempts to memorialize his

brother, to incorporate and inscribe his dead brother onto his own body, and find closure for his mourning.

According to Nancy Berns, finding closure is a new way of mourning over death and grief (Berns 3), a concept that embodies our response to the trauma of loss. Although there is no definitive definition of closure, it is described as a process of coming to terms with loss and grief, finding peace, healing, forgiveness and above all, justice (Berns 2). Closure is an attempt to find a resolution to all these questions. Finding closure is advised for those who are emotionally hurt and aggrieved to help them through their moments of grief and mourning. It is helpful for people, like Booker, who may bemoan and grieve for their beloved ones to such an extent that they become the victims of self-pity. Booker fails to find closure because of inappropriate mourning, burial and lack of justice. His failed mourning or melancholia testifies to the social injustice he cannot come to terms with. According to Schwab, "Fantasies of a replacement child and their unconscious enactment betray a form of failed mourning that operates through a logic of substitution" (Schwab 15). Booker's rose tattoo in memory of his brother expresses his desire to immortalize his brother by denying his loss and erasure from his life. Adam was such a consummate replacement for his stillborn twin brother that following his death, Booker had no soul mate: "Both were dead" (115). Like a dead man walking, he is unable to mourn properly, as he is haunted by the death of his stillborn twin brother, and refuses to accept the death of Adam, whom he identifies as his replacement. He thinks that justice has not been done to his beloved brother, and wants his family to respect and remember Adam. His family perceives his excessive outburst of mourning as an attempt to outmourn them, while his brothers Favour and Goodman think that Booker "wanted a statue of a brother who died when they were babies" (125). The rest of the family see his expression of mourning and grief as "manipulation—as trying to control them—outfathering their father" (125). The family thinks that Booker is acting in grief and melancholy so that he can judge them as lacking in grief. They fail to understand that Booker displays the melancholic's refusal to let the lost object go into the realm of oblivion. Booker is not just mourning his dead brother but the loss of innocence itself—the very reflected embodiment of divine purity.[7]

The Pedagogy of Mourning

Again, Freud is important for understanding the politics of mourning. According to Freud, mourning is not just an act of mourning over the physical loss of a person, but of compromised ideals or shared ideologies, even an abstraction (Secret 142). In Booker's case, the loss of his brother is all the more grievous because sibling love is the purest and most innocent form of love, that requires an angel's love to express it or its reciprocal innocence (160). Booker does not want the memory of his brother to recede into oblivion and wants his family to remember him too. His desire to monumentalize his brother is an attempt at finding closure. Only Booker's aunt, Queen, understands the underlying angst of her nephew. She reaffirms his need to keep the memory of his brother alive and the psychological necessity of working through his grief and mourning: "Don't let him go," [. . .]. Not until he is ready. Meaning, hang on to him tooth and claw. Adam will let you know when it's time" (117). Queen understands the reparative aspect of complete mourning and realizes that Booker will gradually be able to recover after he separates himself from his sense of loss. Mourning erodes the sense of loss with the passage of time. According to Freud, mourning is successful and comes to an end gradually after the subject finds a new libidinal object. Attachment to the lost object is gradually abandoned, especially after the subject is emotionally spent and overcomes his/her sense of loss, finding a replacement or substitute for the lost object (Ricciardi 23). After the temporal phase of mourning is over, when the subject loses interest in everything other than the lost object, and reality-testing shows the object no longer exists, the subject can re-enter the world of relationships with other objects (Ricciardi 24–5). Booker fails to work through his melancholic hang-up. He is unable to overcome his melancholia and rehabilitate himself. Queen's advice to Booker of a gradual recovery from feelings of loss and perpetual state of mourning is evocative of Freud's observation on the impact of mourning on the aggrieved:

> I do not think there is anything far-fetched in presenting it the following way. Reality-testing has shown that the loved object no longer exists, and it proceeds to demand that all the libido be withdrawn from its attachments to that object. . . . Normally, respect for reality gains the day. Nevertheless, its orders cannot be obeyed at once. They are carried out bit by bit, at great expense of time. . . . Each single one of the memories and expectations in which the libido is bound to the object is brought up and hyper-cathected, and the detachment (Losung) of the libido is accomplished in respect of it.
>
> (qtd. in Ricciardi 25)

According to Freud, one of the aims of mourning is to sever the libidinal attachment to the lost object (Gana 25). Mourning is not complete until the object of love is thoroughly de-cathected (Secret 154) and is achieved bit by bit until the libido separates from the lost object (Ricciardi 25). Freud describes the work of mourning as a slow and gradual process, requiring necessary "expenditure of energy" for a renewed interest in life (Ricciardi 28). Only when the subject is able to work through mourning is s/he able to invest elsewhere. The Freudian completion of mourning is when the mourner successfully detaches himself or breaks free of his attachment to the love-object or loss. After the subject has grieved enough, decathexis is over, allowing him/her to carry on free of his/her attachment to the lost object (Min "Remains to be Seen" 232). If the gap caused by the loss of the love-object is not filled, replacement of the cherished object is impossible (Ricciardi 33). According to Freud:

> Although we know that after such a loss the acute state of mourning will subside, we also know we shall remain inconsolable and will never find a substitute. No matter what may fill the gap, even if it be filled completely, it nevertheless remains something else. And actually this is how it should be. It is the only way of perpetuating that love which we do not want to relinquish.
>
> (qtd. in Ricciardi 32)

The Freudian process of mourning is a gradual movement toward forgetfulness or the overcoming of loss, which does not work for Booker. He remains steadfast to the memory of his brother. As Freud observes, "the libido clings to its objects and will not renounce those that are lost even when a substitute lies ready to hand" (qtd in. Ricciardi 29–30). Instead of letting go of the lost object, living through his moment of grief and mourning and finding closure, Booker becomes melancholic and preserves the memory of his brother. Freud cautions us against mourning where the subject is inseparably attached or fixated upon his/her lost love-object (Gana 48). Booker incorporates it into his ego, introjects his brother so much that he becomes a permanent incorporation as a phantom, a dead-alive other in his body (Min 235; Miller "Absolute Mourning" 16). Abraham and Torok call keeping alive the love-object a fantasy of the exquisite corpse/incorporation, internalizing part of the love-object into one's own body (Tuggle "The Haunting of (un) Burial" 64): "Reconstituted from the memories of words, scenes and affects, the objectal correlative of loss is buried alive in the crypts as a full-fledged person, complete with his own topography" (Abraham & Torok 130). The beloved corpse of Adam inhabits the body of the living brother, Booker, in a parasitic relationship. Queen describes this moment of possession and reminds Booker to leave his melancholy and move on by letting go of Adam: "You lash Adam to your shoulders so he can work day and night to fill your brain. Don't you think he is tired? He must be worn out having to die and get no rest because he has to run somebody else's life" (156). This textual description of lashing the body to shoulders is remarkably similar to Derrida's account of how the human body is mourned in *The Ear of the Other*:

> in normal mourning [introjection] . . . I take the dead upon myself, I digest it, assimilate it, idealize it, and interiorize it. . . . This is what Hegel calls interiorization which is at the same time memorization-an interiorizing memorization (Erinnerung). . . . But since it is an *Erinnerung*, I interiorize it totally and it is no longer other.
>
> (qtd. in Secret 151)

Gabriele Schwab's understanding of Nicolas Abraham's concept/vision of the crypt, involves a hidden psychic space in which the subject buries "unspeakable events or unbearable, if not disavowed, losses or injuries" (Schwab 3). She adds that people harbor an undead ghost in this crypt or psychic tomb and they do not want to let them die (Schwab 3). The crypt is "an effect of failed mourning: it is a burial place inside the self for a love-object that is lost but kept inside the self like a loving corpse. The crypt is a melancholic, funereal architectonic in inner space, built after traumatic loss" (Schwab 45). Booker becomes the crypt by mourning and brooding over the death of his brother. He tries to convince his family, especially his parents "to think of some sort of memorial for Adam" (124). His siblings Favor and Goodman think that Booker wants to erect a "statue of a brother who died when they were babies" (125). Nobody seems to realize the logic behind Booker's desire to memorialize the memory of his brother.

Memorials are sites of remembrance and resistance. They bear symbolic witness to struggles for justice. Lack of a memorial, especially in the post-racial context, bespeaks lack of justice and a continued history of abuse and violence against black communities, especially young black boys and men. Lack of mourning and monuments shows disregard for black life and serves to perpetuate and legitimize violence. Booker sees his family's and society's lack of concern for a public memorial as "the savage absence not only of Adam but of himself" (125). In fact, in the context of post-racialism, the absence of a memorial stands for absence of justice and links the brutal murder of Adam to the violence and murders of young black men like Mike Brown and Trayvon: "Another little black boy gone. So?" (114). Behind the fictional disappearance/death of Adam and his discovered bodily remains, there is the gendered legacy of the unresolved grief, unacknowledged and unmourned losses of other parents, whose children disappeared without a trace or justice (Neal 65). Society failed to take account of the larger picture of the event, making for the perpetuation and continuation of civic, judicial and racial injuries (McIvor ch. 1).

This history of social injustice, racial wounds, disregard for black lives, unaccounted for deaths and violence will continue to perpetuate social injustice if not acknowledged or redressed (Tillet 135). Booker cannot come to terms with the loss of his brother or the unmourned loss of other black boys, which exposes a racially biased justice/penal system (Singleton "Introduction"). The disappearance of one black boy brings in its wake a history of unresolved social grief over the disappearance of other black boys. The disappearances of little boys stand for the gendered legacy of unresolved racial violence and abuse, and lack of closure or justice (Singleton ch.2). Booker's racial melancholia and protestations suggest that non-recognition or forgetting, which is a lapse of justice, has become a marker of racial discrimination, lack of civic or legal enfranchisement. His clamor for public acknowledgement and memorialization seeks to redress the ongoing "post-civil rights paradox of African-American legal citizenship and civic estrangement" (Tillet 145). Booker's melancholy is "a result of and in resistance to an enduring struggle with racial oppression" (Singleton ch. 2). His militant melancholia demands the justice and reparation due unaccounted for black boys, a demand for social justice and reconciliation for the elimination of institutional racism (Tillet 136). Booker's mind is haunted by the loss of those little boys who disappeared without trace, and whose unmourned deaths call for collective remembrance and memorialization. To use Morrison's expression, they should not be unaccounted for or disremembered. The disremembered stands for collective racial experiences, unmourned social loss, forgetfulness and national amnesia. In fact, they call for acknowledgement, justice and memorialization. Memorials not only create space for remembrance, but they also highlight struggles for justice. Memorials can help reconcile us with the loss of precious lives and consider how we can address violence in order to engage and dislodge practices of violence and child abuse. They are monuments to human endurance of violence and the lack of justice thereof, a repudiation of forgetfulness and passivity. Memorials call for action and responsibility, social awareness and mobilization, to fight for rights and justice. Lack of memorials signifies the "disremembered and unaccounted for" and lack of justice, how black victims of sexual abuse and violence are forgotten and the perpetrators of violence are either never brought to face justice or unfairly acquitted: "How could they pretend it was over? How could they try to forget and just go on? Who and where was the murderer?" (117).

Compromise, forgetfulness, silence over the loss of precious lives and the failure to recognize them is like giving up the struggle for justice. According to David McIvor, the silence surrounding personal and historical trauma is "a heavy silence, a wounding silence" (McIvor ch. 1). In his inconsolable melancholy, Booker takes on what he considers to be the entire family's and society's incapacity to mourn—and let go of—his brother and countless other young boys. Booker's melancholy is the result of the gendered and "transgenerational effect of unmoored social loss" (Singleton ch. 2). Silence on behalf of the family constitutes not only their inability to mourn but also their inability to seek justice. Like most families who are victims of injustice, they seal off their pain and keep it buried, while Booker is tormented by the desire to do justice to the memory of his brother. Following Derrida on the concept of justice, it is this call for justice which makes Booker live in "the upkeep" or the companionship of his brother and his memory (Secret 171). In the light of the deaths of his innocent brother and those victims of abuse, Booker's call for mourning, public monument, recognition, redress and social justice is understandable. Mourning and monumentalization are not only a way of keeping the memory of a person alive, but also the prerequisite for healing the trauma of loss. Only Queen understands his psychological need to keep the memory of his dead brother alive and the need to mourn properly before letting him go. Queen also understands Booker's psychological need to give up mourning and redirect his energies into loving someone else in the present (Wyatt 178). As a result of her advice, Booker finds living and loving Bride "really good" (157). Booker's love for Bride also relieves him of the melancholic depression and his trauma of loss, which kept him enshrouded after the loss of his brother, Adam:

> Each time he imagined her eyes glittering toward him [. . .] he felt not just a swell of desire but also the disintegration of the haunt and gloom in which for years Adam's death had clouded him.
>
> (131–2)

However, their brief episode of "six months into the bliss of edible sex, free-style music, challenging books and [. . .] the fairy-tale castle collapsed into the mud and sand on which its vanity was built" (135). Booker runs away upon learning Bride was intent on doing a good turn to the presumed pedophile Sofia Huxley, to appease her conscience. Booker's mind is already haunted by the unanswered questions about his dead brother and the disappearances of other black boys. In Booker's eyes, Bride's desire to empathize with Huxley puts her with the victimizer rather than the victim. It makes her at one with his family and society, who are indifferent, resigned and seem to turn a blind eye to crimes of sexual abuse. Bride, however, refuses to accept the position of victim abandoned by her man (Wyatt 183). She finally confronts Booker to ask why he "walked out" on her without any justification. Booker retorts her with his own question: "First you tell me why you bought presents for a child molester—in prison for it, for Christ's sake. Tell me why you sucked up to a monster" (153). She explains why she lied and helped convict Huxley on charges of child abuse while she was innocent, and how she wanted to "make amends" for the wrong she did Huxley in order to gain her mother's affection (153). This strikes a conciliatory note in Booker's heart, who thought she was forgiving a predator like the freak who murdered his brother Adam. Bride and Booker reconcile with each other. Bride confesses her sins and feels newborn. Booker, too, realizes his error of spending a lifetime sitting "on a throne and identify[ing] signs of imperfections in others" (160). He apologizes to his brother for having enslaved him (166). Like Frank and his sister Cee in *Home*, he learns to respect and honor the memory of his dead brother by letting him rest in peace, rather than erecting an eternal tomb inside his own body.[8] Instead of controlling his brother, he finally lets go of his melancholic hold over his dead brother, or what Jean Wyatt describes as "the pride of a melancholic" (Wyatt 180). Both Booker and Bride achieve their moments of epiphany, which Morrison defines as a journey from ignorance to knowledge and enlightenment.

Notes

1. Children become the mirror-image of the pedophile's projected desires and endorse the Freudian child with perverse sexuality or confirm the "doctrine of infant depravity," that children are inherently sexual and sinful. In *God Help the Child*, this view is at odds with the competing view that children are innocent and need protection. See also Robin Bernstein's *Racial Innocence: Performing American Childhood from Slavery to Civil Rights* on the competing portrayals of children as sexually depraved and innocent.
2. Like Booker's democratic response to loss, he wants to address the issue of child abuse in a similar fashion.
3. Claudia Rankine also emphasizes the need to "keep mourning an open dynamic" (150). She reads the Black Lives Matter movement in the same vein, emphasizing the need to keep mourning an open culture as long as black people live in a constant state of existential precariousness and vulnerability. See Rankin's essay "The Condition of Black Life Is One of Mourning."
4. Alfred Frankowski reads mourning and memorialization as a process of "getting history right" (30). The killing and disappearance of children requires public acknowledgement. According to Frankowski, memorialization can help maintain mourning as an open dynamic, providing us with justice, reconciliation and redress. See Frankowski's excellent work *The Post-Racial Limits of Memorialization* on the need to have public monuments to reconcile the wounds of history and violence. Frankowski's views agree with Morrison on the need to have public monuments to honor those who are "unaccounted" and "disremembered." Morrison has voiced the need to honor the dead in numerous interviews including "A Bench by the Road: *Beloved* by Toni Morrison." In this interview Morrison lamented the lack of monuments honoring the dead: "There is no place you or I can go, to think about or not think about, to summon the presences of slaves;

nothing that reminds us of the ones who made the journey and of those who did not make it. There is no suitable memorial or plaque or wreath or wall or sky-scraper lobby [. . .]. There is no small bench by the road" (44). These powerful words inspired the Toni Morrison Society to inaugurate the Bench by the Road project to honor and memorialize the people who sacrificed their precious lives.

5. Having come across and read Claudia Rankine's essay, it is important for me to emphasize that I am drawing historical parallels or analogies with a couple of the most pivotal acts of mourning in American history, which resulted in the Civil Rights movement and the Black Lives Matter movement. Although Rankine has enumerated the mothers of men, like Mobley, Martin, Brown and Eric Garner to mention a few, and the mothers of girls like Rekia Boyd and Aiyana Stanley-Jones, each of whom was a victim of police violence; it is the loss of their precious lives which makes them partake in the discourse of public mourning (Rankine 153–44).

6. According to Rankine, some of McSpadden's neighbors did not want to monumentalize Brown's death because "They didn't need a constant reminder of the ways black bodies don't matter to law enforcement officers in their neighbourhood" (Rankine 153).

7. Booker seems to have a Platonic/Romantic concept of childhood, which endows children with innate goodness and innocence. Such a concept is historically located, inspired by visions of the Romantic poets and the Anglo-American legal systems, which have fostered and nurtured it (Stockton *The Queer Child* 30). This idea of childhood innocence goes against the Calvinistic "doctrine of infant depravity," which means children are inherently sexual and sinful. The doctrine of infant depravity was reversed in the late eighteenth and early nineteenth century, inspired by the Romantic poets' representation of children as innocent angels, able to redeem the adult world. American sermons and child rearing pamphlets were inspired by such visions. Thus, childhood came to be understood "not as innocent but innocence itself; not as a symbol of innocence but as its embodiment. The doctrine of original sin receded, replaced by a doctrine of original innocence" (Bernstein *Racial Innocence* 4). According to Stockton, "the innocent child is the normative child—or the child who, on its path to normativity, seems safe to us and whom we therefore safeguard at all cost" (*The Queer Child* 30). The normative child, who evokes eternal and original innocence, is the measure against which adult life must be defined (31). Therefore, the child who is vulnerable to abuse has to be sheltered and protected. From Booker's point of view, this innocence is lost to him and to the world he inhabits. Hence, he feels the need to protect it.

8. The tragic scene of Queen's death and her funeral, which is celebrated privately and quietly, can be understood in the context of maturity Booker has received. Booker's trumpet tribute for Queen was "off-key and uninspired" and he threw the trumpet in the stream as if, symbolically, he had come to terms with the reality that "Queen [. . .] could die" (173).

Conclusion
Apostrophe in *God Help the Child*

Hear a tua mãe. (*A Mercy*)

Prayer is a central trope in the recent works of Toni Morrison like *A Mercy* and *God Help the Child*. It offers mothers the medium of words to communicate with or touch their daughters. Prayer is one perspective from which we can read the entire beings of motherly figures and their self-sacrificing motivation in Morrison's oeuvre. Prayer puts into perspective the caring thoughts and gestures of mothers, perceived as prayers, intended for the welfare of daughters. The whole being of a good mother embodies the epitome of maternal care. The mother's existence can be defined and read in terms of prayer. One of the most powerful and evocative examples of a mother as the embodiment of prayer comes from *Song of Solomon*. Ruth explains to Milkman how she prayed for the wellbeing of her son day and night: "And I also prayed for you. Every single night and every single day. On my knees" (127). There are similar examples of maternal care and affection in *A Mercy* and *God Help the Child*. The final sections of both these novels are presented through the prayerful perspective of mothers and the power of evocation. The efficacy of evocation and of prayer resides in its ability to put mothers in telepathic contact with daughters, which captures the moments of apostrophe in Morrison's fiction.

According to Miller, "In an apostrophe the speaker breaks off the constative discourse and turns to address some "you" directly, someone either present or absent" ("Glossing the Gloss" 33). He adds, "An apostrophe personifies the "you" to whom it is addressed" as in the form of address in Romantic poetry like William Wordsworth's "The Boy of Winander" ("Glossing the Gloss" 34). Morrison is a poet of apostrophe. J. Hillis Miller, a theorist of genres written in the medium of apostrophe, associates apostrophe with forms of prosopopeia or prosopopeitic discourses (*Versions* 5, 238). Prosopopeia also becomes the ideal medium through which the dead can participate in the lives of the living "by being invoked as an example of sacrifice and suffering" (Stow 19). This principle of prosopopeia brings the discourse of the suffering child invoked by the epigraph of the novel. In fact, applying the logic of this prosopopeitic discourse invokes the epigraph Freud inscribes to *The Interpretation of Dreams*: "What have they done to you poor child?" (qtd. in Cameron 285) as he deals with stories of shocking child abuse just as Morrison does in *God Help the Child*. Discussing the poetics of address in Derrida's *The Postcard*, Miller claims that the overall style of "Envoys" or the Postcard "can be taken as an extended apostrophe, an interpellation of the you that reads" ("Glossing the Gloss" 33). Similar examples of this "extended apostrophe" can be found in *Jazz*, when the narrator, commenting upon the intricate design of city life, directly addresses the reader as "you" (116–120).

Expanding upon his argument Miller concludes, "The whole of 'Envois' can be read as a huge extended apostrophe," sustained by the pervasive use of familiar "tu" (you) in the letters ("Glossing the Gloss" 34). This recipient of the letter or prayer, the reader of the novel "becomes the apostrophised addressee [. . .] with all the responsibilities to respond and decide that Derrida so much insists on" ("Glossing the Gloss" 34). The invocation of "O" is characteristic of an apostrophe just like the invocation of "O Lord" is a signifier of prayer. Morrison's fiction, like a Poe short story, is emblematic of prosopopeia, whereby living beings discourse with dead people or their spirits. It is characteristic of Morrison's late fiction of apostrophe, in which a person tries to address someone else—an absentee—and renders an explanation. For Missy Dehn Kubitschek, the final scene between Heed and Christine in *Love* is "a kind of telepathic communication that signals a return to girlhood closeness" (Kubitschek "Playing in the Wild" 142). The same can be said about the ending of *Sula*. In *God Help the Child*, it comes in the form of an apology, an apostrophe, a plea and a prayer on behalf of and by the mother, Sweetness. According to Kevin Quashie,

> Inherent in prayer is the idea of self as audience; that is, the praying subject speaks to a listener who is manifest in his or her imagination [. . .]. The emphasis in the prayer is not so much on the deity who is listening as it is on the subject who is praying and his or her capacity and faithfulness. In this way, prayer reflects the most perfect communication—to speak to one who is and is not one's self. This excellent conversation exposes the praying self as both needy and capable.
>
> (Quashie *The Sovereignty of Quiet*)

Black women are allegedly demonized for not protecting their children, while almost all of Morrison's mothers make personal sacrifices in the interests of their children. They are motivated by the desire to protect their children, keep them out of harm's way in a place of safety as is the case with Sethe from *Beloved*, a mina maé from *A Mercy* and Sweetness in *God Help the Child*. Prayer embodies a life of attention, commitment, devotion, responsibility and sacrifice against the odds of life and institutionalized slavery. Prayer embodies an intersubjective exchange between mothers and daughters. It gives expression to maternal love. It is an intense moment of passion during encounters of call and response between humans and the divine and between mothers and daughters. Although there has been considerable progress in race relations, Sweetness reflects on her past deeds as a mother whose motivation was "well-intended"—under the circumstances and the "necessary way"—to bring up her daughter. Her prayer is a performative act of speech directed at her daughter in the hope of being understood. Like Morrison's other mother figures, she resorts to the best course of action for her daughter as a mother. Her tough upbringing produces the good future of her daughter. Now that her own daughter is going to be a mother, she hopes that her daughter will realize that responsible motherhood is challenging, involving more than "cooing, booties, and diapers" (178). Responsible motherhood makes sure that the child is prepared for life and all its challenges. Sweetness, as a mother, utilizes prayer to invoke and reinforce in her daughter the power to perform her duties as a responsible mother who nurtures and protects her child. During her intense moment of prayer, the abstraction or synecdoche of the child as an object or repository of prayer "affords a slippage from individual to society, from the child to the nation, from the lost to the true, authentic self; and—most significant in relation to the child sexual abuse"—from being vulnerable to being the traumatized victims of sexual abuse who are in need of protection (Burman "Childhood" 42). The motherly appeal "God help the child" also draws connections between mothers and daughters in the rest of Morrison's oeuvre and the readers to the site of spiritual connection with the author. This final prayer in the novel is reminiscent of the prayer in *Love* when Sandler, described as the "othermother" by Pelagia Goulimari, prays for Roman and cautions him against the dangers of escorting a sporting woman: "God help the boy if he got soul-chained to a woman he couldn't trust" (112).

The potential success of Sweetness' prayer resides in its ability to make telepathic contact with her daughter so that it can affect the desired transformation in her daughter, enabling her to become accountable as a mother. Sweetness' prayer revolves around gratitude for a new life and looks at the possibility of a radically new future, of a future that might be different from the past. It conceptualizes a future (though still a prayer of hope) similar to the wish made by the baby's parents for a life, for a new creation free from oppression, slavery, racism and abuse of all kind: "A child. New life. Immune to life or illness, protected from kidnap, beatings, rape, racism, insult, hurt, self-loathing, abandonment. Error-free. All goodness. Minus wrath" (175). She says amen to that: "Good luck and God help the child" (178), ending her address on this note of tikvah. According to Elie Wiesel, "TIKVAH MEANS HOPE and hope is represented by children. It is they who must justify our hope in education, in human relations, and social justice. In other words: they represent our hope in a future which is an improvement on our past" (Wiesel iv). Morrison positions the ideal of the child at the center of the struggle for a more just society in which there is no racial or sexual abuse and more democratic and equitable distribution of societal benefits and justice, irrespective of skin color or skin privilege, especially in societies that have a history of racial oppression.

Bibliography

Abraham, Nicolas and Maria Torok. *The Shell and the Kernel: Renewals of Psycho-analysis*, Volume 1. Chicago: U of Chicago P, 1994. Print.

Akhtar, Jaleel. *Dismemberment in the Fiction of Toni Morrison*. Newcastle upon Tyne: Cambridge Scholars, 2014. Print.

Anderson, Melanie R. *Spectrality in the Novels of Toni Morrison*. Knoxville: U of Tennessee P, 2013. Print.

Asante, Molefi Kate. "Blackness as an Ethical Trope: Toward a Post-Western Assertion." *White on White/Black on Black*. Ed. George Yancy. Lanham: Rowman & Littlefield Publishers, Inc., 2005. Print.

Babb, Valerie. *Whiteness Visible: The Meaning of Whiteness in America Literature and Culture*. New York: New York UP, 1998. Print.

Baker, Houston A. and Merinda K. Simmons. *The Trouble with Post-blackness*. New York: Columbia UP, 2015. Print.

Barnaby, Andrew. *Coming Too Late: Reflections on Freud and Belatedness*. New York: State U of New York P, 2017. Print.

Battersby, Matilda. "Oprah Winfrey 'Victim of Racism' in Switzerland: Billionaire Told She Can't Expensive Handbag at Exclusive Zürich Store." *Independent*, 9 August 2013. www.independent.co.uk/arts-entertainment/tv/news/oprah-winfrey-victim-of-racism-in-switzerland-billionaire-told-she-cant-afford-expensive-handbag-at-8753660.html/.

Bennett, Juda. *The Passing Figure: Racial Confusion in Modern American Literature*. New York: Peter Lang Publishing, 1996. Print.

———. "Toni Morrison and the Burden of Passing Narrative." *African American Review*, Vol. 35, No. 2, Summer 2001, pp. 205–217.

———. *Toni Morrison and the Queer Pleasure of Ghosts*. Albany: State U of New York P, 2014. Print.

Berns, Nancy. *Closure: The Rush to End Grief and What It Costs Us*. Philadelphia: Temple UP, 2011. Print.

Bernstein, Robin. *Racial Innocence: Performing American Childhood from Slavery to Civil Rights*. New York: New York UP, 2011. Print.

Bonilla-Silva, Eduardo. *Racism Without Racists: Color-Blind Racism and the Persistence of Racial Inequality in America*. Lanham: Rowman & Littlefield Publishers, 2014. Print.

Burman, Erica. "Childhood, Sexual Abuse and Contemporary Political Subjectivities." *New Feminist Stories of Child Sexual Abuse: Sexual Scripts and Dangerous Dialogues*. Eds. Paula Reavey and Sam Warner. London: Routledge, 2002. Print.

Cameron, Olga Cox. "From Tragic Fall to Programmatic Blueprint: 'Behold This Is Oedipus. . .'." *Clinical Encounters in Sexuality: Psychoanalytic Practice & Queer Theory*. Eds. Noreen Giffney and Eve Watson. New York: Punctum Books, 2017. Digital.

Caruth, Cathy. *Unclaimed Experience: Trauma, Narrative, and History*. Baltimore: Johns Hopkins UP, 1996. Print.

Chen, Angela. "Toni Morrison on Her Novels: 'I Think Goodness Is More Interesting'." *The Guardian*, 4 February 2016. www.theguardian.com/books/2016/feb/04/toni-morrison-god-help-the-child-new-york/.

Childs, Erica Chito. *Fade to Black and White: Interracial Images in Popular Culture*. Lanham: Rowman & Littlefield Publisher, 2009. Print.

Collins, Patricia Hill. *Black Feminist Thought: Knowledge, Consciousness, and the Politics of Empowerment*. New York: Routledge, 1991. Print.

Crawford, Margo Natalie. *Black Post-Blackness: The Black Arts Movement and Twenty-First-Century Aesthetics*. Urbana: U of Illinois P, 2017. Digital.

———. *Dilution Anxiety and the Black Phallus*. Columbus: Ohio State UP, 2008. Print.

———. "Natural Black Beauty and Black Drag." *New Thoughts on the Black Arts Movement*. Eds. Lisa Gail Collins and Margo Natalie Crawford. Piscataway: Rutgers UP, 2006. Print.

———. "What Was *Is*: The Time and Space of Entanglement Erased by Post-Blackness." *The Trouble with Post-Blackness*. Eds. Baker A. Houston and Merinda K. Simmons. New York: Columbia UP, 2015. Print.

Davis, Angela Y. "Black Women and Welfare." *Intersectionality: A Foundations and Frontiers Reader*. Ed. Patrick R. Grzanka. Boulder: Westview Press, 2014. Print.

DeSalvo, Louise. *Virginia Woolf: The Impact of Childhood Sexual Abuse on Her Life and Work*. London: The Women's Press, 1991. Print.

Dickie, Margaret. *Stein, Bishop & Rich: Lyrics of Love, War & Place*. Chapel Hill: U of North Carolina P, 1997. Print.

Dolezal, Rachel. *In Full Color: Finding My Place in a Black and White World*. Dallas: BenBella Books, Inc. 2017. Digital.

Dreisinger, Baz. *Near Black: White-to-Black Passing in American Culture*. Amherst: U of Massachusetts P, 2008. Print.

Du Bois, W. E. B. *The Souls of Black Folk*. Seattle: Amazon Classics, 2017. Digital.

Dyson, Michael Eric. *The Black Presidency: Barack Obama and the Politics of Race in America*. New York: Houghton Mifflin Harcourt, 2016. Digital.

Elam, Michele. *The Souls of Mixed Folk: Race, Politics, and Aesthetics in the New Millennium*. Stanford: Stanford UP, 2011. Print.

Elan, Priya. "Why Pharrell Williams Believes in the New Black." *The Guardian*, 22 April 2014. www.theguardian.com/music/shortcuts/2014/apr/22/trouble-with-pharrell-williams-new-black-theory/.

Ellis, Trey. "The New Black Aesthetic." *Callaloo*, No. 38, Winter 1989.

Fabi, M. Giulia. *Passing and the Rise of the African American Novel.* Urbana: U of Illinois P, 2001. Print.

Fanon, Frantz. *Black Skin, White Masks.* London: Pluto P, 2008. Print.

Farrington, Lisa E. *Creating Their Own Image: The History of African-American Women Artists.* New York: Oxford UP, 2005. Print.

Fleetwood, Nicole R. *On Racial Icons: Blackness and the Public Imagination.* New Brunswick: Rutgers UP, 2015. Print.

———. *Troubling Vision: Performance, Visuality, and Blackness.* Chicago: U of Chicago P, 2011. Digital.

Foreman, Katya. "Grace Jones: Style, Power and In-your-face Sexuality." *BBC Culture.* www.bbc.com/culture/story/20151002-grace-jones-style-power-and-in-your-face-sexuality.

Frankowski, Alfred. *The Post-Racial Limits of Memorialisation: Toward a Political Sense of Mourning.* Lanham: Lexington Books, 2015. Digital.

Fuller, Hoyt W. "Towards a Black Aesthetics." *Within the Circle: An Anthology of African American Literary Criticism from the Harlem Renaissance to the Present.* Ed. Angelyn Mitchell. Durham: Duke UP, 1994.

Fultz, Lucille P. "*Love*: An Elegy for the African American Community." *Toni Morrison: Memory and Meaning.* Eds. Adrienne Lanier Seward and Justine Tally. Jackson: U of Mississippi P, 2014. Print.

Gallego, Mar. "*Love* and the Survival of the Black Community." *The Cambridge Companion to Toni Morrison.* Ed. Justine Tally. Cambridge: Cambridge UP, 2007. Print.

Gana, Nouri. *Signifying Loss: Toward a Poetic of Narrative Mourning.* Lewisburg: Bucknell UP, 2011. Print.

Gates, Henry Louis, Jr. and Gene Andrew Jarrett. *The New Negro: Readings on Race, Representation, and African American Culture, 1892–1938.* Princeton: Princeton UP, 2007. Print.

Goldberg, Jesse A. "From Sweetness to Toya Graham: Intersectionality and the (Im)Possibilities of Maternal Ethics." *Toni Morrison on Mothers and Motherhood.* Eds. Lee Baxter and Martha Satz. Bradford: Demeter Press, 2017. Digital.

Goulimari, Pelagia. *Toni Morrison.* London: Routledge, 2011. Print.

Guinier, Lani and Gerald Torres. "Political Race and the New Black." *The New Black: What Has Changed—And What Has Not—With Race in America.* Eds. Kenneth W. Mack and Guy-Uriel E. Charles. New York: The New Press, 2013. Print.

Hall, Alice. *Disability and Modern Fiction: Faulkner, Morrison, Coetzee and the Nobel Prize for Literature.* Hampshire: Palgrave MacMillan, 2012. Print.

Hart, David William. "Dead Black Man, Just Walking." *Pursuing Trayvon Martin: Historical Contexts and Contemporary Manifestations of Racial Dynamics.* Eds. George Yancy and Janine Jones. Lanham: Lexington Books, 2013. Digital.

Henry, Paget. "Whiteness and Africana Phenomenology." *What White Looks Like: African-American Philosophers on Whiteness Question.* Ed. George Yancy. New York: Routledge, 2004. Digital.

Hobbs, Allyson. *A Voluntary Exile: A History of Racial Passing in American Life.* Cambridge, MA: Harvard UP, 2014. Digital.

Hobson, Janell. *Body as Evidence: Mediating Race, Globalizing Gender*. Albany: State University of New York P, 2012. Print.

———. *Venus in the Dark: Blackness and Beauty in Popular Culture*. New York: Routledge, 2005. Print.

hooks, bell. *Black Looks: Race and Representation*. Toronto: Between the Lines, 1992. Print.

———. *Salvation: Black People and Love*. New York: HarperCollins Publishers, 2001. Print.

James, Robin. *Resilience and Melancholy: Pop Music, Feminism, Neoliberalism*. Winchester: John Hunt Publishing, 2015. Digital.

Johnson, Patrick E. *Appropriating Blackness: Performance and the Politics of Authenticity*. Durham: Duke UP, 2003. Print.

———. *No Tea, No Shade: New Writings in Black Queer Studies*. Durham: Duke UP, 2016. Digital.

Jones, Janine. "Tongue Smell Color Black." *White on White/Black on Black*. Ed. George Yancy. Lanham: Rowman & Littlefield Publishers, Inc., 2005. Print.

Judy, Ronald A. T. "Fanon's Body of Black Experience." *Fanon: A Critical Reader*. Eds. Lewis R. Gordon, T. Denean Sharpley-Whiting and Renée T. White. Oxford: Blackwell Publishers, 1996. Print.

Kennedy, Randall. *Sellout: The Politics of Racial Betrayal*. New York: Pantheon Books, 2008. Print.

Kincaid, James R. *Erotic Innocence: The Culture of Child Molesting*. Durham, NC: The Duke UP, 1998. Print.

Kubitschek, Missy Dehn. "Playing in the Wild: Toni Morrison's Canon and the Wild Zone." *Toni Morrison: Forty Years in the Clearing*. Ed. Carmen R. Gillespie. Lewisburg: Bucknell UP, 2012. Print.

Lee, Shayne. *Erotic Revolutionaries: Black Women, Sexuality, and Popular Culture*. Lanham: Hamilton Books, 2010. Digital.

Li, Stephanie. "Black Literary Writers." *The Trouble With Post-Blackness*. Eds. Baker A. Houston and K. Merinda Simmons. New York: Columbia UP, 2015. Print.

———. *Signifying Without Specifying: Racial Discourse in the Age of Obama*. New Brunswick: Rutgers UP, 2012. Digital.

Locke, Alain. *The New Negro*. New York: Touchstone, 1999. Digital.

Mack, Kenneth W. and Guy-Uriel E. Charles (eds.). *The New Black: What Has Changed—And What Has Not—With Race in America*. New York: The New Press, 2013. Print.

Martin, Reginald. *Ishmael Reed and the New Black Aesthetic Critics*. New York: St. Martin's Press, 1988. Print.

Mccaskill, Barbara. "Twenty-First-Century Literature: Post-Black? Post-Civil Rights?" *The Cambridge Companion to Civil Rights Literature*. Ed. Armstrong, Julie. New York: Cambridge UP, 2015. Print.

McIvor, David W. *Mourning in America: Race and the Politics of Loss*. Ithaca: Cornell UP, 2016. Digital.

Melancon, Trimiko. *Unbought and Unbossed: Transgressive Black Women, Sexuality and Representation*. Philadelphia: Temple UP, 2014. Print.

Mercer, Kobena. "Black Hair/Style Politics." *Welcome to the Jungle: New Positions in Black Cultural Studies*. Ed. Mercer Kobena. New York: Routledge, 1994. Print.

Miller, Alice. *Thou Shalt Not Be Aware: Society's Betrayal of the Child*. New York: A Meridian Book, 1984. Print.

Miller, J. Hillis. "Absolute Mourning: It Is Jacques You Mourn For." *Re-reading Derrida: Perspectives on Mourning*. Eds. Tony Thwaites and Judith Seaboyer. Lanham: The Rowman & Littlefield Publishing, 2013. Print.

———. "Glossing the Gloss in 'Envoys' in *The Post Card*." *Going Postcard: The Letters of Jacques Derrida*. Ed. Vincent W. J. van Gerven Oei. New York: Punctum Books, 2017. Digital.

———. *Versions of Pygmalion*. Cambridge: Harvard UP, 1990. Print.

Mills, Charles W. *Blackness Visible: Essays on Philosophy and Race*. Ithaca: Cornell UP, 1998. Digital.

Min, Susette. "Remains to Be Seen: Reading the Works of Dean Sameshima and Kahnh Vo." *Loss: The Politics of Mourning*. Eds. David L. Eng and David Kazanjian. Berkeley: U of California P, 2003. Print.

Monahan, Michael J. *The Creolizing Subject: Race, Reason and the Politics*. New York: Fordham UP, 2011. Print.Morrison, Toni. "Author Toni Morrison Presents Her Latest Book, 'God Help the Child: A Novel'." Interview by Charlie Rose, 30 April 2015. https://charlierose.com/videos/23790/.

———. "Bench by the Road: *Beloved* by Toni Morrison." *Toni Morrison: Conversations*. Ed. Carolyn C. Denard. Jackson: UP of Mississippi, 2008. Print.

———. *The Bluest Eye*. New York: Vintage Books, 2007. Print.

———. *God Help the Child*. New York: Alfred A. Knopf, 2015. Print.

———. "An Interview with Toni Morrison." With Bessie W. Jones and Audrey Vision. *Conversations with Toni Morrison*. Ed. Danille K. Taylor-Guthrie. Jackson: UP of Mississippi, 1994. Print.

———. *Jazz*. New York: Vintage, 2004. Print.

———. *Love*. New York: Vintage, 2005. Print.

———. *The Origin of Others: The Charles Eliot Norton Lectures, 2016*. Cambridge, MA: Harvard UP, 2017. Digital.

———. "The Pain of Being Black." Interview With Bonnie Angelo. *Conversations with Toni Morrison*. Ed. Danille K. Taylor-Guthrie. Jackson: UP of Mississippi, 1994. Print.

———. *Tar Baby*. New York: Vintage, 2004. Print.

———. "Toni Morrison in Conversation." Conversation with Mario Kaiser and Sarah Ladipo Manyika. *Granta*, 29th June 2017. https://granta.com/toni-morrison-conversation/.

Murray, Derek Conrad. *Queering Post-black Art: Artists Transforming African-American Identity After Civil Rights*. London: I. B. Taurus & Co, 2016. Print.

Neal, Mark Anthony. *Soul Babies: Black Popular Culture and the Post-Soul Aesthetic*. New York: Routledge, 2002. Print.

Nerad, Julie Cary. *Passing Interest: Racial Passing in US Novels, Memoirs, Television, and Film, 1990–2010*. Albany: State U of New York P, 2014. Digital.

Norman, Brian. "The Dilemma of Narrating Jim Crow." *The Cambridge Companion to Civil Rights American Literature*. Ed. Julie Armstrong. New York: Cambridge UP, 2015. Print.

O'Dell, Lindsay. "The 'Harm' Story in Childhood Sexual Abuse: Contested Understandings, Disputed Knowledge." *New Feminist Stories of Child Sexual Abuse:*

Sexual Scripts and Dangerous Dialogues. Eds. Paula Reavey and Sam Warner. London: Routledge, 2002. Print.

Oforlea, Aaron Ngozi. *James Baldwin, Toni Morrison and the Rhetoric of Black Male Subjectivity*. Columbus: The Ohio State University. 2017. Digital.

Osucha, Eden. "Passing in Blackface: The Intimate Drama of Post-Racialism on *Black. White.*" *Passing Interest: Racial Passing in US Novels, Memoirs, Television, and Film, 1990–2010*. Ed. Julie Cary Nerad. Albany: State U of New York P, 2014. Digital.

Patterson, Orlando. "The Post-Black Condition." *The New York Times*, 22 September 2011. www.nytimes.com/2011/09/25/books/review/whos-afraid-of-post-blackness-by-toure-book-review.html/.

Peterson, Christopher. *Bestial Traces: Race, Sexuality, Animality*. New York: Fordham UP, 2013. Print.

Pfeiffer, Kathleen. *Race Passing and American Individualism*. Amherst: U of Massachusetts P, 2003. Print.

Quashie, Kevin. *The Sovereignty of Quiet: Beyond Resistance in Black Culture*. New Brunswick: Rutgers UP, 2012. Print.

Rankine, Claudia. "The Condition of Black Life Is One of Mourning." *The Fire This Time: A New Generation Speaks About Race*. Ed. Jesmyn Ward. New York: Scribner, 2016. Print.

Reed, Ishmael. *The Reed Reader*. New York: Basic Books, 2000. Print.

Ricciardi, Alessia. *The Ends of Mourning: Psychoanalysis, Literature, Film*. Stanford: Stanford UP, 2003. Print.

Scarry, Elaine. *On Beauty and Being Just*. Princeton: Princeton UP, 1999. Print.

Schwab, Gabriele. *Haunting Legacies: Violent Histories and Transgenerational Trauma*. New York: Columbia UP, 2010. Print.

Schwarcz, Lilia Moritz. "Painting and Negotiating Coors." *"I Don't See Colour": Personal and Critical Perspectives on White Privilege*. Ed. Bettina Bergo. University Park: Penn State UP, 2015. Print.

Secret, Timothy. *The Politics and Pedagogy of Mourning: On Responsibility in Eulogy*. London: Bloomsbury, 2015. Digital.

Shavers, Rone. "Fear of a Performative Planet: Troubling the Concept of 'Post-Blackness'." *The Trouble With Post-Blackness*. Eds. Baker A. Houston and Simmons K. Merinda. New York: Columbia UP, 2015. Print.

Shoenfeld, Jené. "Can One Really Choose? Passing and Self-Identification at the Turn of the Twenty-First Century." *Passing Interest: Racial Passing in US Novels, Memoirs, Television, and Film, 1990–2010*. Ed. Julie Cary Nerad. Albany: State U of New York P, 2014. Digital.

Singleton, Jermaine. *Cultural Melancholy: Readings of Race, Impossible Mourning, and African American Ritual*. Urbana: U of Illinois P, 2015. Digital.

Stereo, Williams. "Common, Pharrell, and 'The New Black': An Ignorant Mentality that Undermines the Black Experience." *Daily Beast*, 19 April 2015. www.thedailybeast.com/common-pharrell-and-the-new-black-an-ignorant-mentality-that-undermines-the-black-experience/.

Stern, Katherine. "Toni Morrison's Beauty Formula." *The Aesthetics of Toni Morrison: Speaking the Unspeakable*. Ed. Marc C. Conner. Jackson: U of Mississippi P, 2000. Digital.

Stockton, Kathryn Bond. *Beautiful Bottom, Beautiful Shame: Where "Black" Meets "Queer."* Durham, NC: Duke UP, 2006. Print.

———. "The Queer Child Now and Its Paradoxical Global Effects." *The Child Now* (A Journal of Lesbian and Gay Studies). Eds. Julian Gill-Peterson and Kathryn Bond Stockton. Durham, NC: Duke UP Books, 2016. Print.

———. *The Queer Child: Or Growing Sideways in the Twentieth Century.* Durham: Duke UP, 2009. Print.

Stow, Simon. *American Mourning: Tragedy, Democracy, Resilience.* Cambridge: Cambridge UP, 2017. Digital.

Taylor, Keeanga-Yamahtta. *From #BlackLivesMatter to Black Liberation.* Chicago: Haymarket Books, 2016. Digital.

Taylor, Paul C. *Black Is Beautiful: A Philosophy of Black Aesthetics.* Pondicherry: Wiley-Blackwell, 2016. Digital.

———. *On Obama.* New York: Routledge, 2016. Digital.

———. "Post-Black, Old-Black." *African American Review*, Vol. 41, No. 4, Winter 2007, pp. 625–640. Digital.

Thompson, Barbara. *Black Womanhood: Images, Icons, and Ideologies of the African Body.* Seattle: U of Washington P, 2008. Print.

Thompson, B. Lisa. *Beyond the Black Lady: Sexuality and the New African American Middle Class.* Urbana: U of Illinois P, 2009. Print.

Tillet, Salamishah. *Sites of Slavery: Citizenship and Racial Democracy in the Post-Civil Rights Imagination.* Durham, NC: Duke UP, 2012. Digital.

Touré. *Who Is Afraid of Post-blackness: What It Means to Be Black Now.* New York: The Free Press, 2001. Print.

Tuggle, Lindsay. "The Haunting of (un) Burial: Mourning the 'Unknown' in Whitman's America." *Re-reading Derrida: Perspectives on Mourning.* Eds. Tony Thwaites and Judith Seaboyer. Lanham: Rowman & Littlefield Publishing, 2013. Print.

Vanzant, Iyanla. "Bump, Grind, Twist, and Celebrate." *Naked: Black Women Bare All About Their Skin, Hair, Hips, Lips, and Other Parts.* New York: Berkley Publishing Group, 2005. Print.

Walker, Rebecca. *Black Cool: One Thousand Streams of Blackness.* Berkeley: Soft Skull Press, 2012. Print.

West, Cornel. *The Cornel West Reader.* New York: Basic *Civitas* Books, 1999. Print.

Wiesel, Elie. *Tikvah: Children's Book Creators Reflect on Human Rights.* New York: SeaStar Books, 2001. Print.

Wilkinson, Claude. "Appropriating Blackness: Oreo Dreams Deferred in Charles Fuller's a Soldier's Play." *Constructing the Literary Self.* Ed. Patsy J. Daniels. Newcastle upon Tyne: Cambridge Scholars Publishing, 2013. Print.

Willet, Cynthia and Julie Willett. "Trayvon Martin and the Tragedy the New Jim Crow." *Pursuing Trayvon Martin: Historical Contexts and Contemporary Manifestations of Racial Dynamics.* Eds. George Yancy and Janine Jones. Lanham: Lexington Books, 2013. Digital.

Winters, Joseph R. *Hope Draped in Black: Race, Melancholy and the Agony of Progress.* Durham, NC: Duke UP, 2016. Digital.

Wyatt, Jean. *Love and Narrative Form in Toni Morrison's Later Novels.* Athens: U of Georgia P, 2017. Print.

Yancy, George. *Black Bodies, White Gazes: The Continuing Significance of Race.* Lanham, MD: Rowman & Littlefield Publishers, Inc., 2008. Print.

———. *What White Looks Like: African-American Philosophers on Whiteness Question.* New York: Routledge, 2004. Digital.

——— (Ed.). *White on White/Black on Black.* Lanham, MD: Rowman & Littlefield Publishers, Inc., 2005. Print.

Zackodnik, Teresa C. *The Mulatta and the Politics of Race.* Jackson: UP of Mississippi, 2004. Print.

Ziegler, Kortney. "Black Sissy Masculinity and the Politics of Disrespectability." *No Tea, No Shade: New Writings in Black Queer Studies.* Ed. E. Patrick Johnson. Durham, NC: Duke UP, 2016. Digital.

Index